PRAISE FOR
THE RESTAURANT MARKETING MINDSET

"Few people in the world understand restaurants strategically—even fewer know how to leverage marketing effectively. Chip is one of them. The combination of practical and theoretical understanding offers unique insights."

MARTIN LINDSTROM, *New York Times* bestselling author of *Buyology* and one of *Time* magazine's 100 Most Influential People

"Chip has done it. He's put a comprehensive, tactical strategy into digestible actions in an easy-to-absorb playbook. It's a must-read book full of must-apply tactics for any restaurant leader."

JOSEPH SZALA, founder of Vigor and author of *The Bullhearted Brand*

"I own restaurants in San Diego, and I am constantly looking to connect with the brightest minds in hospitality marketing. Chip has a top industry podcast and is asked to speak at all the top events because he is one of those minds. Chip is also a master of the craft of teaching storytelling to restaurant professionals. Reading this book will transform how you look at investing in marketing for your business!"

SHAWN WALCHEF, founder of Cali BBQ Media

"The reader benefits from Chip's broad and extensive career and the subsequent lessons he learned—not only from his professional experience, but also from the coaching of owner/operators across the US. Knowing the purpose of the enterprise is central to success; Chip guides you through the process seamlessly."

JAMES C. WILLIAMSON, PhD, LTC Hospitality Solutions Board of Directors

"Chip Klose has a ground-up understanding of restaurant operations. He has taken that experience—coupled with his uncanny ability to synthesize and simplify concepts and ideas into something that can be solved—and become a restaurant marketer of remarkable acumen. In this book you get both his experience and a pathway to marketing your concept."

BRET CSENCSITZ, owner of Gotham New York

THE
RESTAURANT
MARKETING
MINDSET

www.amplifypublishinggroup.com

The Restaurant Marketing Mindset: A Comprehensive Guide to Establishing Your Restaurant's Brand, from Concept to Launch and Beyond

For more information, please contact:
Amplify Publishing, an imprint of Amplify Publishing Group
620 Herndon Parkway, Suite 220
Herndon, VA 20170
info@amplifypublishing.com

Library of Congress Control Number: 2023905190

CPSIA Code: PRV0623A

ISBN-13: 978-1-63755-756-3

Printed in the United States

For my son, Preston.
Everything changed the moment you arrived.

THE
RESTAURANT
MARKETING
MINDSET

A Comprehensive Guide to
Establishing Your Restaurant's Brand,
from Concept to Launch and Beyond

CHIP KLOSE

an imprint of Amplify Publishing Group

CONTENTS

PART THREE
EXTERNAL MARKETING

PART FOUR
PUTTING IT TOGETHER

INTRODUCTION

W hy do you want to own a restaurant? I ask because the numbers are pretty grim. According to *FSR* magazine, 60 percent of restaurants don't make it a year, and 80 percent shutter within five.[1] Our industry operates with razor-thin profit margins, and as labor and food costs continue to rise, the statistics become ever more depressing. In a way my goal is to try to talk you out of opening a restaurant altogether. Because we don't need *just another* restaurant. In fact, we don't need *just another* anything. What we do need is something bold and interesting, dare I say . . . something original.

Now let me be clear: I'm not suggesting that every town should get their own Alinea. But we also don't need *just another* burger joint. We've got plenty of those already, many of which we've come to know and love. These days we don't have the luxury of putting out a newer version of something people already have, and so I'm going to challenge you to create the kind of place no one has ever seen before—the kind of place that exists only in your imagination.

Anything less isn't worth your time. More importantly, it isn't worth our money.

I've spent the last twenty-two years working in hospitality and have the scars to prove it. I know all about eighty-hour workweeks and the stress that comes from opening restaurants in one of the most saturated markets in the world. I live here in New York City, where I've spent my entire adult life collaborating with some of the biggest names in the culinary world. I've opened Michelin-starred restaurants and collaborated with James Beard Award–winning chefs. I've hosted American presidents, international celebrities, clueless tourists, and the "regular people" who make up the majority of our nightly reservation books. While there is no one-size-fits-all approach to running a successful restaurant, there are things that all great restaurants have in common. The first of which is originality—either in concept, execution, or the way they position themselves in the market. Simply put, originality provides the only clear path to success. And for that we need a plan. More to the point, we need a *strategy*.

The ideas in this book can be applied to any product, service, or experience, but I've focused on restaurants because it's where my passion lies. I also believe it's an industry in desperate need of an overhaul. It doesn't matter if you're doing quick-service Mexican out of a storefront in Tempe or running the fanciest wine bar on Kiawah Island; the ideas I lay out will work for you. Read it the right way and this book will shift the way you think about hospitality and provide new tools and tactics to help ensure future success.

If you're feeling a bit apprehensive about any of this, then great! It means you're serious about the work and are ready for the journey ahead. (To be honest, I'd be more concerned if you weren't nervous.) The path forward isn't easy, and so if you're not up to the challenge, better to know that now. Close the book, return it to the shelf, and choose a different line of work. I mean it. Go find another industry—one that's a bit more forgiving—because it's impossible to succeed anymore unless you're all in. For those of you still reading, I say welcome! We're a passionate group of chefs, owners, operators, and marketers all committed to helping the people we serve.

I've laid out the book in a deliberate way, stacking the concepts one on top of the other. We start small and build out from there. You'll also notice that the book will constantly invite you to participate. Fans of the *Restaurant Strategy* podcast will know that it's not enough to just follow along and nod your head in agreement. The only real way to create lasting change is to take action. You'll find exercises at the end of each chapter intended to help you implement the ideas while they're fresh instead of waiting to finish the book. It's the best way I know to make sure you're putting these things into practice. Of course, you can blow past all of them. But then I'd ask: Why did you pick this book up in the first place? The answer, I hope, is that you believe in yourself and your business and that you're committed to building a profitable enterprise. Assuming those things are true, I say: What have you got to lose?

The worst fate I can imagine for this book is that it sits on the shelf collecting dust. Instead, I want you to dirty it up. Crease the spine and underline passages that resonate with you. Dog-ear pages, scribble notes in the margins, and highlight anything you think can be applied to your own business. Finally, pass the book along to the people you work with. Or, better yet, get them their own copy. Not because it helps me sell more books, but because that simple act will transform your business. Collaboration, you'll soon come to see, is another important ingredient to success.

To help you get where you're going, I'll point you toward a free resource I've created—*The Restaurant Marketing Mindset Workbook*—which was designed to be a companion to this book. It's available as a free PDF download by visiting TheRestaurantMarketingMindset.com/workbook. Print it out, throw it in a binder, work your way through as you read this book, and by the end you'll have all your work collected in one place. It follows along exactly with this book and is a great way to hold yourself accountable.

I hope you'll agree that one of the best aspects of the job is how we get to build rich communities. The *Restaurant Strategy* podcast—and by extension this book—is no different. It's about connecting dedicated professionals from all around the world, and I consider myself lucky to be at the center of those conversations. Like any great maître d', let me welcome you by raising a glass. I'm thrilled you found us and even more excited that we found you.

Cheers!

PART ONE
THE FOUNDATION

CHAPTER 1
WHAT IS MARKETING?

Before we do anything else, I want to agree on a definition for marketing. Ready? It comes down to just three questions:

What is the product?
Who is it for?
How can we reach them?

That's it, the simple three-step recipe we'll return to time and time again as we continue along on our journey. As you'll see in the pages ahead, marketing is about serving an audience. There are nuances, of course, but for our purposes at this early stage, I want you to keep repeating those three questions like a mantra: *What is the product? Who is it for? How can we reach them? . . . What is the product? Who is it for? How can we reach them? . . . What is the product? Who is it for? How can we reach them? . . .*

Historically, marketers have typically followed one of two paths:

FIND A CUSTOMER FOR THE PRODUCT
or
MAKE A PRODUCT FOR THE CUSTOMER.

While they both offer a way forward, only the latter will consistently lead to success. You identify a problem, then craft a specific solution to that problem. Unfortunately, what we see most often in our industry is the first approach: someone opens a restaurant, then tries to figure out who might want to eat there.

Be warned: this path often leads to something I call the *Field of Dreams* effect. I'm sure you remember the 1989 film starring Kevin Costner about an Iowa corn farmer who hears a voice telling him, "If you build it, they will come." That voice seemed to suggest that if the farmer cleared his cornfield and turned it into a baseball diamond, a bunch of once-great, long-dead ballplayers would arrive night after night to play nine innings of first-class baseball. In time, the voice promised, crowds would arrive to watch those games, and the family's shaky financial situation would be all but secured. And of course that's exactly what happens, and it's a wonderful, feel-good movie, but I'm sorry . . . I hope we can all agree that it's a ludicrous plot. If you saw that story on the nightly news, you'd laugh at the guy and talk about how crazy he was for digging up half his crop. So why, then, does this seem to be the thought process for so many restaurant owners? "If I build it, they will come."

The simple fact is—they won't. Diners have too many options these days. Places they've come to rely on, with dishes they've grown to love, in dining rooms that feel as familiar as their own homes.

If you're offering a product, you better know who that product is for. You better know who else is trying to serve that same audience. And you better be able to articulate how this new product—in this case, your restaurant—is a better solution to a diner's problem than what they currently have. That, in a nutshell, is the challenge all marketers face.

Again, repeat after me: *What is the product? Who is it for? How can we reach them?*

How many chefs dream of opening their own place, only to watch it end in disaster? All too often their menu seems to say, "It's my turn . . . my opportunity to cook the kind of food I've always wanted to cook." And as their focus turns inward, they slowly forget about one key piece of the equation—the people they're supposed to be serving. Think about how ludicrous that would be in other industries. What if a painter ignored your request and simply splattered your living room walls with the color *they* thought would look best? Or if a cab driver took you uptown instead of downtown simply because that was the direction *they* were headed? Or if the woman at the deli counter handed you half a pound of cheddar even though you had clearly ordered swiss?

Without our guests we have no business. And so it doesn't matter how innovative the menu is, how precisely the service is executed, or how beautiful the dining room may be. None of it matters unless someone walks in. And that's the lesson most restaurateurs learn the hard way. It's not just about what you're able to create, but rather what the guest is willing to pay for. Again: *What is the product? Who is it for? How can we reach them?* The guest is literally at the center of our definition for marketing, which is great because we are in the service industry, after all. But when you let them slip from that position, everything else falls apart.

Now wait, you may be thinking! A few pages back this guy was extolling the virtues of originality, and now suddenly he's saying that the reason restaurants fail is that chefs often get too big for their britches. And so let me pause here to clarify. You can open the fanciest, most ostentatious restaurant in town, but before you do, you've got to make sure there's an audience for that. In fact, the sky's the limit when it comes to what's *possible*, but the guest will tell you what's *probable*. Meaning, it's *possible* that you could find success running a fine dining restaurant in Dayton, Ohio, serving a twenty-two-course tasting menu for $500 a head. But it may not be *probable*. Only by understanding your market will you come to discover who needs to be served and in what ways. Old school marketing textbooks refer to this as finding a customer's *pain point*.

So yeah, there may be a group of wealthy individuals in Dayton, Ohio, who are dying for the kind of high-end experience typically found only in larger markets. Great! You've found an audience with a pain point. But note the difference. Instead of just plowing ahead with some expensive offer, you've assessed the market and found a product that your audience actually needs. From here on out, you'll see that all our conversations will begin by identifying the *who*. Who is this for? Who needs to be served? Who has a problem that needs solving?

Once we know our audience, we can then begin crafting solutions to their problems. In business, a solution often comes in the form of goods or services. That is true for just about any line of work you can think of. Plumbers solve a specific problem for the people they serve; so does an airline company. Apple, Starbucks, Marriott, Lululemon, Oscar Mayer, and more. All of them offer goods or services geared toward a specific audience—specific solutions to a specific set of problems. The same is true with your restaurant. At its purest, you are crafting a solution to someone's problem. So, then, what exactly are we selling? Well, this may seem counterintuitive, but I want to share the first of a series of shifts I'll be asking you to make:

> **MINDSET SHIFT**
> We don't sell food; we sell experiences.

If people just wanted something to eat, there are certainly cheaper options out there. After all, a can of beans costs about a dollar at the supermarket. Two cans, some chicken, and a bag of rice feeds a family of four for less than fifteen bucks. It's not a particularly interesting meal, but if someone simply needs *to eat,* they can find sustenance for much less than it costs to dine at your restaurant. So let's assume people aren't in survival mode when they walk in your front door.

Remember, too, that a restaurant offers so much more than just what the guests put in their mouths. The service is an important aspect of what you're offering. You are, after all, preparing the food for your guests, bringing it to them, then cleaning up afterward. The decor needs to be considered as well. Music, lighting, and design are all part of the experience you're crafting. In fact, everything— from the restaurant's website to the parking lot to the signage, menus, service, plating, and final bill—is all part of the overall dining experience and must be factored in when we talk about your *product.* The question then becomes: What kind of product are you selling? Meaning, what experience are you crafting? There is no wrong answer as long as you stay focused on the consumer.

Again, remember our definition for marketing. Keep repeating those three questions in your head.

People spend years studying marketing—earning expensive degrees from prestigious universities—and still don't come out with a definition as clean and straightforward as the one I just gave you. Don't be fooled by the big words and fancy acronyms; marketing is simple, and as Leonardo da Vinci famously wrote, "Simplicity is the ultimate sophistication." Which leads us to another important concept:

MINDSET SHIFT
There is a difference between *simple* and *easy*.

My goal, both on the *Restaurant Strategy* podcast and in writing this book, is to take complicated marketing concepts and make them both understandable and actionable. What good is an Ivy League education if you don't know how to put it to use? The concepts should be simple to understand, because rarely (if ever) are they easy to implement. We should spend our time incorporating the ideas, not struggling to understand them.

So if all marketing can be defined by those three questions—*What is the product? Who is it for? How can we reach them?*—then it's worth noting something important: the *who* and the *what* will almost never change, while the *how* will change all the time. The Yellow Pages has given way to Google. Travel agents have been replaced by Expedia. And can you even remember a world without social media?

Before we can talk about tactics, though, we need to put together a strategy. We're going to start with something I call the ABCDs of Marketing. This *simple* framework will provide the foundation for just about everything else we'll discuss. What are the ABCDs?

Audience
Brand
Competition
Differentiation

We'll spend a chapter on each one, and by the time we get to the other side, you should have a pretty good idea of what your product is, who it's for, and what other restaurants are vying for the same dollars you're trying to capture. Most importantly, you'll discover ways to stand out in a noisy marketplace and translate that into repeat diners and higher check averages.

ASSIGNMENT #1

I want you to begin by answering the three questions that make up our definition for marketing. Literally, I want you to describe the product you sell. Then I want you to identify who that product is for. Finally, I want you to list all the ways you reach your audience. We will go into all of this in greater detail in the coming chapters, but this is an important place to start. Remember, you can download the free workbook by visiting TheRestaurantMarketingMindset. com/workbook.

CHAPTER 2

A IS FOR AUDIENCE

Who is your restaurant for? And please don't say *everyone*. It is not for everyone. Not even close. For starters, 99 percent of the world's population has never even heard of your restaurant, nor can they easily get to your restaurant. There's a large number of people that can't afford your restaurant and an even larger group who won't like the food you serve. So immediately we've identified something like seven and a half billion people who won't ever dine with you simply due to geography, preference, or cost. And that's good news. Great news, in fact!

MINDSET SHIFT
Sometimes the best way to figure
out who your product is for . . .
is to first figure out who it is *not* for.

You may resist at first, but I am going to convince you that in order to go big, you have to think small. I'm talking about getting specific, niching down to find a group of patrons who desperately wants what you have.

Every market has a *population*, which includes all the people in a given area. Here in New York City, we have a population of roughly eight million people.[2] While it would be great to make a restaurant that would attract all of them, I know that's simply not possible. So if I were to open a new restaurant here in town, I would need to find a way to segment the population. What we're looking for is a *target audience*. There are many different ways to divide up a population, but I'm going to introduce you to four of them. Remember, you're trying to figure out what your audience has in common; do that and you can figure out what problem you're uniquely qualified to solve.

If you're a locksmith, you're trying to help the guy down the street get back into his house. If you park your ice cream truck next to the playground, you're treating the neighborhood kids to delicious frozen snacks on a hot summer day. All great products are the answer to someone's prayer, so the question is: Whose prayers are you answering?

Empathy is a word a lot of marketers use these days, and for good reason. We must put ourselves in our customers' shoes. Whom are you serving? What are their struggles? And how can you make their lives better? Remember what I said: to go big, you must think small. What follows are four ways for segmenting a population to not only find your *target audience* but better understand the unique ways they need to be served.

DEMOGRAPHICS

All markets are made up of different demographics—groups of people that can be divided up by age, sex, race, religion, income, education, occupation, and more. And while this isn't always the most productive way to determine who your audience is, it certainly is one way to do it. For example, let's say you're going to open a sports bar. You'll have wall-to-wall TVs broadcasting all kinds of live sporting events, with burgers and wings on the menu and a list of thirty different beers on tap. I think we'd all assume that the key demographic is probably men, which isn't to say that women won't dine there, because they will! But if you had to target a specific audience just by demographic, I think you'd admit that a majority of your customers will probably be men. It's a fine place to start.

But let's go one step further and see if we can't get a bit more specific. Imagine you're going to open this sports bar in a college town like Ann Arbor, Michigan. While it's easy to imagine a bunch of undergrads wandering through the quad, the population on gameday is somewhat more diverse. In fact, while the University of Michigan has tens of thousands of full-time students, it's also home to a large population of professors, administrators, and other staff who work in and around the campus. And on Saturdays the campus also fills up with thousands of alumni and parents. So if we had to narrow down our audience beyond simply men, what might be a good way to do it? I might suggest dividing our men into two different groups: the ones who have money (faculty, staff, alumni) and the ones who don't (students). Simply speaking, we've got the "haves" and "have-nots." Dividing up our population like this will help us decide which of those two audiences we wish to target—literally, whether we'll be serving two-dollar pints of Bud Light or twelve-dollar cans of craft IPA. Understanding the demographics of your particular market can give you a sense of what their needs are and provide you with insights to better serve them.

PSYCHOGRAPHICS

If demographics describe *who* the buyer is, then psychographics explain *why* they buy.

It's about studying people according to their attitudes, aspirations, and other psychological criteria. Simply put, this is where we focus on the mindset of our audience. What are their hopes and dreams? Their fears? What gives them pleasure? What sorts of values help guide their buying decisions?

In certain instances it may be more productive to target your audience based on demographics, but not always. Other occasions require us to scratch way below the surface. In the example I just used, we divided our population into two distinct groups: the "haves" and the "have-nots." If we decide to pursue the upscale sports bar, we will undoubtedly have to divide up our audience further. Just because a professor can afford a twelve-dollar beer doesn't necessarily mean they are going to order one. We use psychographics to discover new things about our potential audience. In this case, we want to find people who believe what we believe: that small-batch craft breweries are creating a product that is not only superior to cheaper mass-produced beer, but is worthy of the higher price tag. We want people who appreciate quality, artistry, and diversity of taste. To succeed we'll need to identify the "haves" who also believe that quality beer is worth paying for. Remember what I said at the top of the chapter: we often figure out who our product is for simply by identifying who it is not for.

GEOGRAPHY

Also think about geography as it pertains to your audience. Literally, where do they live? What kind of neighborhood? Is it urban, sub-urban, or rural? How far do they have to travel to get to you? How exactly do they get there? Car? Train? Plane? Boat? How difficult is that journey? Is the meal worth the effort? Is it good enough to recommend to their friends, family, and neighbors, even if it is somewhat inconvenient? The time and energy it takes actually has a lot to do with their overall dining experience, so bear that in mind.

Next I want you to think about what kind of home they live in. Is it an apartment or a house? Do they rent or do they own? Is that their only home or one of many? Is any of that important when it comes to their decision-making? Perhaps not, but if you're in a Florida beach town catering to wealthy snowbirds, your approach may differ from how you might communicate with some of the residents who live there year-round. Understanding the role geography plays simply helps us get a clearer picture of who your audience is, which ulti-mately helps us understand how your restaurant fits into their lives.

BEHAVIOR

Following that line of thinking, I want you to consider their behavior. And by that I mean what are their likes and dislikes? What are their interests? Do they have hobbies? If they're single, how might that inform your marketing? What if they're married? Do they have kids? How old are those kids? Parenting a four-year-old is different than parenting a fourteen-year-old, so get specific.

We certainly touched on some of this when we talked about demographics, but here we're taking that information and making a set of further observations. For example, if demographics is about identifying your audience's income level, and psychographics explains what matters to our audience, then understanding their behavior will show us exactly what they do with their spare time and discretionary income. Consider the other restaurants they frequent. What other ways do they spend their money? Have you considered how much free time they have each week and what they typically do with that free time? Understanding all of that will give you a leg up on your competition and help you to better serve your audience.

———

Finally, then, you're going to use all that information to determine what sorts of pain points your audience has. Keep this in mind:

> **MINDSET SHIFT**
> Our audience is not here to solve our problems;
> we exist to solve theirs.

On the podcast I tell a personal story to make this point. I live in Brooklyn, New York, though not in a particularly cool part of the borough. Our neighborhood is safe, our apartment is spacious, and we're just a quick subway ride away from Manhattan, but we don't really have much in the way of culture. No bars, restaurants, cafés. No nightlife to speak of. There's nowhere to get a good burger on a Friday night, let alone a decent glass of wine. And certainly there's nothing around here that I would call a good date spot.

However, my son goes to school just a couple of miles away—five subway stops from our house in a much more vibrant neighborhood—and there are five or six great restaurants within a block of his school. In fact, the best of the bunch is right next door to his school. I trust that some of the parents reading this will recognize our plight: My wife and I both work full time, and over the past couple of years, there have been plenty of occasions when we've had to race out of work just to get him in time. It's sometimes 5:30 or 6:00 p.m. by the time we scoop him up from his after-school program. We're tired, hungry, and eager for a quick win—which is how we've often wound up at the restaurant just next door to the school.

And wouldn't you know—most nights the tables are filled with other parents dining with their children. My son's school is home to a diverse population—different cultures, income levels, and backgrounds—and so you can't segment us by mere demographics. Yet we all share a specific set of behaviors, geography, and psychographics. Looking at the other families around the dining room, I recognize that we're all in a similar predicament. We all have to pick up our kids at the end of a long day, and perhaps their neighborhoods are devoid of good dining options as well. And so our pain point is the same: we are tired and hungry and long for a civilized meal with our kids—one that might include a well-made craft cocktail. This restaurant has recognized that and succeeds largely because they deliver on the promise.

In the end, all of this is meant to help you identify your audience's pain point. The couple down the street needs a romantic place to celebrate their tenth anniversary, and the guy next door who's always running late needs a convenient spot to grab a bagel and coffee on his way to the office. You are the solution to someone's problem; it's your job to figure out what problem you're uniquely qualified to solve. Figure that out and your business will change almost overnight.

> **MINDSET SHIFT**
> Understanding your target audience is the
> only way to effectively serve them.

We take care of people for a living, and that alone is worth celebrating. I want you to recognize that others couldn't do what you do, and many out there who try don't do it very well. You have built a business on the promise of serving people, so you owe it to them to learn exactly *who they are* and *what they need*. Do that well and all you have to do is tap them on the shoulder and let them know you've got a solution to their problem.

ASSIGNMENT #2

I want you to identify who your audience is. You're going to come up with three or four different personas to figure out who needs what you have. Take a single sheet of paper for each one (remember you can also download the workbook I've created) and start segmenting your audience. For each persona, describe their demographics, psychographics, geography, behaviors, and pain point. As the final piece to this exercise, try to think of someone you know who fits each of the personas you've identified. If it helps, try naming each persona. This often makes the exercise feel more tangible and should help you focus your marketing efforts in the future.

CHAPTER 3

B IS FOR BRAND

If the first step of this framework is about figuring out who you're serving and what sort of problem they have, then the second part is about crafting a solution to that problem. That means understanding the kind of product you're selling, articulating how that product helps your audience, and designing the ways in which you wish to engage with that audience. First-time restaurant owners often skip this step, thinking it's enough to have good food and good service, and expect to turn a profit. It's not. The industry is now at a saturation point, and "good" is no longer good enough. You need to find ways to stand out, to set yourself apart from the competition. You need to know exactly what kind of experience you provide.

For all intents and purposes you are building a brand, and the best ones out there have a strong identity. It stands to reason, then, that you need to establish the same for your brand. Now, before you start to argue, let me assure you that this isn't nearly as difficult as it sounds. There are tons of great examples from which we can draw inspiration. Start by considering some of the products and companies you already love and think about why you've remained so loyal to them over the years. For me I think about Apple, Nikon, and Nike. I've been loyal to each of those companies, returning time and time again when I need to replace an older product with something new. What companies are on your list, and how would you describe the actual experience of interacting with them? I'll use Apple as an example because it's an iconic brand that most of us know. Think of the products themselves, the retail stores, and the website. Think of the feeling you get taking a brand-new iPhone out of its box. (That moment, by the way, is carefully designed by the team in Cupertino.) Then think about the ongoing relationship you have with the products and what they allow you to do. What does the Apple logo stand for, and what sort of emotion does it evoke?

Our interactions with a given brand influence how we feel about the company and its products. A brand, after all, is simply defined as the sum of all the interactions a consumer has with a given company. To define the brand, you have to clarify the following three areas:

THE PRODUCT ON OFFER
Exactly what is it you're selling?

THE BRAND IMAGE
What sort of emotion does the product convey?

AUDIENCE ENGAGEMENT
What is the relationship you wish to have with your customers?

You should aspire to be as unique and well-defined as the best brands on the planet. It is the only way to stand out in a noisy marketplace, and make no mistake—the restaurant industry is every bit as saturated as the car market or consumer electronics. You may not have the reach or resources of a publicly traded company, but in the eyes of the consumer, you are no different. They may not be aware of their biases, but people these days expect certain things from the companies they support. And so you must strive to provide them with that. In the pages that follow, we'll go through each of these three areas separately, then discuss the best ways to integrate them. By the end you'll have a clear understanding of what you're offering, how you should communicate that offer, and the best way to build a long-standing relationship with your target audience.

THE PRODUCT ON OFFER

Food may be the thing we serve, but it's not what we're selling. As I mentioned earlier, the product on offer is the *experience,* and you must be deliberate about the kind of experience you're crafting. For example, are you a romantic date spot or a postwork watering hole? Family-friendly or power lunch? Cheap and easy, or elevated and expensive? Understanding who you are will help you make better decisions—decisions that will attract the right kinds of customers. As you think about the product on offer, really you should be trying to identify the key details of your business. Literally, let's just talk about what you serve and how you serve it.

CUISINE

We can start this exercise with the obvious question: What type of cuisine do you offer? Is it Chinese, American, Mexican, Italian? Greasy bar food or high-end sushi, American classics or something entirely new? Burgers? Seafood? Fusion? What? Define, as best you can, the kind of food you serve at your restaurant. It is, after all, the main draw—best to define it as clearly and succinctly as possible.

LEVEL OF DINING

When it comes to the level of dining, I want you to identify one of the following: quick service, casual, or fine dining. This gives people a sense of what to expect when they come to your restaurant. Let's say you run a Mexican restaurant. Is it a quick-service concept like Chipotle or a high-end affair like Pujol? For the prospective diner, this is an important distinction. The first provides a quick meal on the go, while the second is a celebratory dinner with a loved one. By identifying your level of dining, you're helping to define your product for the consumer. Of course, there's a caveat to this. Over the past twenty years, the lines have become blurred. Chains like McDonald's and Burger King had long defined the quick-service space, but then along comes a company like Panera. There, you order at the register and then wait at a table until someone delivers your food to you. With that simple touch, fast casual was born, exploiting an opportunity to provide something between quick service and casual. Likewise, chefs and restaurateurs have been redefining the fine-dining space for the last two decades. Atomix, Atera, and Chef's Table at Brooklyn Fare are high-end New York City hot spots that all offer multicourse tasting menus for diners who sit at a bar facing in toward the kitchen. David Chang's Momofuku empire serves top-notch riffs on Korean classics but in laid-back surroundings. Olmsted out in Brooklyn serves their dishes family style to the center of the table, helping to tone down the more pretentious aspects of a typical fine dining experience.

PRICE

The cost of a meal often aligns neatly with the level of dining, but not always. To illustrate this point, I'll use another example here in New York City. Midtown Manhattan is home to dozens of fine-dining restaurants all within spitting distance of each other. Specifically, the area is home to three of the city's finest restaurants: one French, one New American, and one Japanese. While they all serve "expensive" tasting menus, there is quite a bit of variance. For example, the French restaurant is currently the cheapest of the bunch, offering a four-course prix fixe for $198 per person. Compare that to the omakase (Japanese) experience just across the street, which begins at $750. The New American restaurant offers their dinner tasting menu for $355 a head. These are three of the city's very best restaurants—all sharing the highest honor a restaurant can garner (the coveted three-star rating in the Michelin Guide)—and each of them has a wildly different price point. Sure they're all "expensive," but I think we can agree that there is a big difference between $198, $355, and $750. Understanding the cost of your product will allow you to better communicate the value you provide your guests. (But more on that later.)

LOCATION

Finally, we've got to talk about location. Geography is often a big part of a restaurant's identity; no doubt that's true for yours as well. So let's define it. What country are you in? What state? What city? Are you right downtown or out in the suburbs? If you're in a city, you'll want to talk about your neighborhood. In most cities, the various neighborhoods have their own unique identity. Undoubtedly, that detail will help define you. Beyond that, think about how people get to you and what that experience is like. If they drive, where will they park? If they take public transportation, what are the closest subway lines and bus routes? Are you situated on the main drag or tucked away on a side street? In the top floor of a high-rise or way down in the basement? Where a restaurant is located is often just as important to a prospective diner as the kind of food that is served.

THE BRAND IMAGE

The best companies in the world excel at connecting with their customers on a visceral level. In fact, most of us consider the brands we support to be part of our identity. That's certainly true for me, and I'm betting it's true for you as well. Most of us align ourselves with brands and products we rely on—companies we take pride in supporting.

What does it say about a person when you see them typing away on a MacBook in their favorite little coffee shop? Likewise, what do you think when you see someone get out of their brand-new Bentley? Or when you see a group of guys in Yankees jerseys enter the bar? Humans are tribal creatures, and affiliation is a powerful tool. By simply understanding that fact, you can begin to harness it to create rabid fans for your own brand.

Your first job, as I've said, is to craft a compelling solution to a specific problem, and then make it clear that you are the most obvious choice. Then you must build a connection with your people so that you are top of mind with the people you most wish to serve. To do that, you should find a way to bring emotion to the table. And guess what? There is no one way to do that.

To get started, look to the brands you already know and love. Car companies do this brilliantly, as do sports franchises. Consumer electronics, more and more, are leaning into this idea of affiliation. And luxury brands have it down to a science. Look carefully at the way they connect with their customers and see what you might be able to apply to your own business.

AUDIENCE ENGAGEMENT

Our audience has a problem, and we want them to know that we have solved it for them. As I just pointed out, we want them to connect with us on an emotional level so that we're top of mind when it matters. The question then becomes how do we engage with them in a meaningful way? Brands do this in all sorts of innovative ways. The key, as I noted a moment ago, is empathy. By putting yourself in your customers' shoes, you will learn a great deal about them. You will discover who they are and what they care about, and that will help you build more lasting relationships with them.

In our increasingly digital world, finding opportunities to make an authentic connection goes a long way. With all the texting we do these days, isn't it refreshing when someone picks up the phone and dials your number? With all the emails we get, isn't it fun when someone actually sends you a letter through the mail? Think about what sort of emotion you wish to evoke and then identify specific opportunities to bring those emotions to life.

Again, if you've crafted a specific solution to someone's problem, you'll want to make sure they realize that you—and you alone—are the answer to their prayers.

———————

Here's a good way to think about all this: Imagine you've just arrived at a dinner party, and you don't know anyone except the host. As you make your way across the room, she turns, greets you with a big hug, and introduces you to a group of people huddled just nearby. She says, "This is the friend I was telling you about, the one who owns that restaurant I love." And the four or five people she's been speaking with suddenly light up with excitement. "What kind of restaurant is it?" they ask. It's a simple question that requires a straightforward answer. So what do you tell them? If you were the owner of Chipotle, you might say, "Well, I own a chain of quick-service Mexican restaurants, where guests get to build their own burritos and bowls." Or what about if you were the owner of Masa in New York City? "It's a high-end sushi restaurant in the heart of Manhattan, where guests are treated to a series of small bites of sliced raw fish." If you ran Blue Hill up in Westchester, New York, you might say, "Well, it's both a farm and restaurant built on the old Rockefeller Estate in Tarrytown, where nearly everything we serve comes right from our own property."

In many ways I'm asking you to come up with an elevator pitch for your restaurant—a quick way to communicate exactly what kind of experience you're offering. It's the first step to defining your brand. Once you've defined it, you then need to communicate how exactly that solves a problem for your audience. In fact, that's what you're going to do every single day from here on out. Your job is to find new and interesting ways to explain what you do and why it matters.

This is an idea that will resurface many more times throughout the book, but I'll introduce it here: don't be afraid to work backward. Figure out how you want people to feel about their meal and then craft an experience that delivers the desired result. Figure out what sort of profit you can expect and then build a business model that can deliver those results. Define the kind of culture you want for your restaurant and then hire people who will fit well into that structure. Nike is an athletic brand that puts performance above all else because it's what their fans crave. They are solving a problem for their audience. Their products exist merely to solve that problem. Armed with that knowledge, they can then craft a brand experience that delivers on that promise. Make no mistake: the same is true with your restaurant.

ASSIGNMENT #3

Write an elevator pitch for your restaurant. Imagine you're at that cocktail party and get introduced to a group of people who don't know anything about you or your establishment. Describe who you are and who your restaurant is for. Explain where you're located and what sort of experience you provide. How are you solving a specific problem for a specific group of people?

CHAPTER 4

C IS FOR COMPETITION

By now you should have a good sense of who your audience is and what their needs are. You should also know what sort of experience you're crafting. Your product—meaning, your restaurant—should answer someone's prayers. Do that consistently and you will have built something that people care about. It's the first step to building a profitable business. The next step is to figure out who else is trying to serve that same audience. We're going to lovingly refer to them as your competitors. And yes, I mean lovingly. In time you will come to love the competition. Why?

> **MINDSET SHIFT**
> Competition does two important things:
> First, it validates your idea. Second,
> it gives you a category.

It stands to reason that before you bring your product to market, you will want to know whether the idea has legs. Is the problem you've identified actually a problem that needs solving? Do your customers recognize your solution as valuable? Are they willing to pay for it? One key way to judge whether your business idea has merit is to look at who else is trying to serve a given audience. Competition provides a certain amount of validation: *you're not the only one who has identified a problem that needs solving.*

The second thing competitors do is to help define your category. It's tempting just to lump together all the restaurants in a given market, but there's a danger in that. Why? Because different restaurants serve different audiences, often at different times of day and for different purposes. For example, if you open a brew pub, you will probably want to be in a category with other bars, maybe even other beer bars—which will actually help you in the long run. The person buying a quick salad to take back to their desk won't find what they're looking for at the brew pub you open. Nor will the couple looking for a quiet place to enjoy a romantic dinner. Being in a category helps you market your product because it helps prospective patrons think of you at times that matter.

That couple celebrating their anniversary makes a list of the most romantic restaurants in town. The executive assistant who doesn't have time for a proper lunch break is triangulating all of the salad spots within a three-block radius. The group of guys looking for a cool place to watch the big game will make a list in their heads of all the best bars in the neighborhood. In many ways a category provides your guests with a "shortlist"; your job is simply to get onto that list.

Another important thing to keep in mind when it comes to categories is that you'll often fit into more than one. Let's say you're going to open that brew pub here in New York City. Just off the top of my head, I can think of three or four different categories you might fall into. You could easily be grouped together with other great neighborhood spots within a certain radius, as well as bars with great beer selections citywide. To go one further, you might be listed in a category that includes best beer bars on the East Coast or in the whole country. Depending on the market you're targeting with a specific piece of communication, you'll decide which category you're going to put yourself into. You'll speak to the folks in your neighborhood one way and the beer lovers in surrounding states another. Why? Because the locals will be attracted by one set of benefits (proximity, convenience, hospitality), while the tourists might focus on others (broad selection, rare finds, bragging rights). If there's anything I want you to notice at this point, it's that specificity is key. Different target markets may be attracted to your restaurant for very different reasons, and those will help define your marketing strategy.

So, then, how exactly do you determine a category (or categories) for your restaurant? There are no rules when it comes to this sort of thing, but there are some guidelines. A good starting place is to look at the areas we discussed in Chapter 3, when we were discussing the identity of your restaurant. For good measure, I'm giving you a few extras as well. In all, I've identified the following seven different ways you might be able to divide up the competition.

LOCATION

This is probably the most obvious way to divide up your market, though keep in mind that location can be interpreted in a bunch of different ways. For example, are you building a list of the best restaurants in the world or just those in Europe? Or maybe you're looking at just one country, like France. Or will you zero in on a single city, like Paris? Perhaps you're creating a list of the best restaurants on the Left Bank or just in the 7th arrondissement or on a specific stretch of the Rue Saint-Dominique. Location can mean many different things, so here I'll urge you to be as specific as possible when trying to identify your competitors by location.

CUISINE

Another obvious way of thinking about your category is to consider some of the other restaurants serving the same cuisine as you. For example, if you're opening an Indian restaurant in town, it might behoove you to identify some of the other great Indian restaurants. If you're a sub shop, you'll want to know how many other sub shops there are. Same thing with barbecue or sushi or Irish pubs. Remember, when people are in the mood for pizza, they compile a list in their heads of their favorite pizza places. Your job is to get your restaurant onto the lists that matter so you can be top of mind when it counts!

LEVEL OF DINING

Another important way you can divide up the competition is by level of dining. Typically a restaurant will fall into one of three categories: quick service, casual, or fine dining. If people are looking for a quick bite after the ball game, they're probably zeroing in on a certain type of experience. Couples looking for a romantic date spot are probably seeking something very different. This is what is meant by level of dining.

PRICE

Of course, price often goes hand in hand with level of dining but not always. Remember earlier when you were trying to articulate the identity of your own restaurant? Now you're going to do the same with your competitors. If you're running a high-end restaurant, you may believe that you're competing with all the other Michelin-starred restaurants in town, but there is often a great deal of variation when it comes to price. A little research will show you where you stack up. You may be quite surprised when you compare your prices with those of your competitors; restaurants you assumed you were competing against may not be competitors after all.

PURPOSE

Are you family-friendly and fun or buttoned-up and aloof? Are you providing quick, tasty meals to tourists in Times Square or high-powered lunches to the bankers on Madison Avenue? Different restaurants serve different purposes. It's possible for an individual to be the target market for a multitude of different concepts but just at different times. Think about yourself for a moment. Where do you go for your morning coffee? If you're like most people, it's different from your go-to lunch spot, which is also different from your favorite postwork watering hole. The kind of restaurant you go to with your friends to watch a ballgame is probably different from the place you'd go to celebrate an anniversary with your spouse. You can't be all things to all people, so do your best to identify what sort of role you fill in your customers' lives.

PEOPLE

Without people, your restaurant is just a big, empty room with an overpriced lease. Your customers and staff breathe life into the space and make it a place worth visiting. It stands to reason, then, that your people may be one key way to categorize your restaurant. For example, is your executive chef female? Perhaps your restaurant will be lumped together with the other notable high-end restaurants with women at the helm. Or do you have a master sommelier running the wine program? There are currently fewer than three hundred in the world; if your restaurant is lucky enough to have one of them, that puts you in an elite category. And don't forget about your patrons. Perhaps you're in the theater district, and so you cater to a bunch of actors, stagehands, or musicians. They will help define you as much as anything else.

CLAIM TO FAME

Do you offer a nightly tasting menu? Are you one of a handful of farm-to-table restaurants in your town? Are you a Spanish wine bar, an authentic omakase counter, a Neapolitan pizza shop? If there's something specific you serve, it may put your restaurant into a category with just a few others. Likewise, do you offer some peculiar dessert or some over-the-top appetizer? Figure out who else is doing something similar. Establish a category for you and those few competitors, and then figure out how to separate yourself from the crowd.

————

Word of mouth is still just as powerful as ever, and whether you like it or not, your customers will do much of the work for you. By identifying a category for yourself, you give them a shorthand—a way to talk about the experience to their friends, family, and colleagues. "We went to this great Italian place, but everything was served family style." Or, "It was this super fancy restaurant, except there's just a single tasting menu that changes nightly." Or, "It was an ice cream shop, but all they had were these unusual flavor combinations."

All of those are real places. In fact, I've been to all of them, and they're among the best culinary experiences I've ever had. In each instance the brand gave me a vocabulary to use, a shorthand to help me share my experience with others. Look carefully, though, and you'll notice that each of those three examples has a specific structure. The first part establishes a category (Italian joint, fine-dining restaurant, ice cream shop); the second then gives some key point of differentiation (family style, tasting menu, unusual flavors). A category is valuable because it narrows down the competition, which in turn helps your audience remember you. In reality, though, it only gets us halfway there. Once we find ourselves listed with a bunch of competitors, it's the marketer's job to create separation. In the next chapter, we're going to talk all about how to differentiate ourselves from the competition. As it turns out, that's the key to unlocking the rest of the book.

ASSIGNMENT #4

Take five blank pieces of paper, and on the top of each one, label the category you're going to put yourself into and then a subheading that provides a bit of context. For example, you might label one page "Location," and then below it you'll write, "Neighborhood bars in the West Village." Or "Cuisine" and then "Chinese restaurants in Schaumburg, Illinois." Then on each page, number one through ten down the left side and identify all the other restaurants you compete with in that specific category. You're going to do that for each of the five pages.

Next you're going to spread the five pages out in front of you, and on a sixth piece of paper, I want you to make a list of any restaurant that appears on more than one page. Of course, it's important to identify all your competitors, but those you're competing with in numerous areas are of particular concern. In the next chapter you'll have to work extra hard to provide some sort of separation from them.

CHAPTER 5
D IS FOR
DIFFERENTIATION

"Tell me a bit about yourself."

How many job interviews start with this same question? While overused, it can also be quite effective because it gives you, the candidate, an opportunity to breathe life into your résumé. The guy sitting across the table is inviting you to craft a narrative, to make sense of the list of responsibilities and job changes you've just handed him. After all, everyone interviewing for the job has an impressive list of accomplishments. What makes one person stand out from another? The candidates are being asked to tell a story, and the one who can tell the best story always wins.

Storytelling is the foundation for all human connection. It's what we do best—how we relate to others and give meaning to the world around us. And the reality is we get some version of that question every single day. You arrive home from work and your wife asks, "How was your day?" Or you're introduced to someone at a party, and they ask, "So what do you do?" No one is looking for a recitation of facts and figures. They want insight, perspective. The truth is people want an excuse to get excited. In marketing we call this a *reason to believe*. What they're looking for is a good story.

In the last chapter we spoke all about the importance of categories. Remember, a category allows you to identify competitors. It validates your idea and helps your prospective customers remember you at opportune times—like when they get hungry. Of course, now that you've got a category, you'll need to find ways to separate yourself from the competition. So how do you do that?

In an interview setting, the ones who get hired are rarely the most qualified. Instead, the best candidates have simply learned how to identify what sets them apart from the other candidates. More than that, they've found a compelling way to communicate it. The same is true in the service industry. The best restaurants lean into the things that make them unique, doubling down on their differentiation points. In marketing textbooks they call this the *value proposition*. In layman's terms, it's the thing that would make a diner choose you over the competition.

And this is something all marketers use regardless of industry. Think about your own buying habits. What kind of car do you drive? Where do you do your banking? What brand of sneakers do you own? What's your favorite soft drink? Favorite sports team? Favorite restaurant? We make decisions every single day about the products we buy and the brands we support, and those decisions aren't random. Most people do some kind of research and consider the alternatives before making a decision, right? To think like a marketer—and that's what you are now—you have to start asking yourself what makes one option more appealing than another.

If you're like most people, you have a favorite pizza place. Can you tell me what makes it stand out in your mind? Try to put your finger on it. Is it the crust, the sauce, the variety of toppings? Or maybe it's the size of the pie, the convenience, or the cost? Maybe it's the simple fact that you know the owner and want to support them. My point is—there is some reason you have (consciously or unconsciously) chosen that pizza place as your go-to. The thing that makes them stand out from all the alternatives is their value proposition.

As you're probably already realizing, different people choose different products for different reasons, which makes a lot of sense. But do you know what's also true? Different people often wind up choosing the *same product* for different reasons. Think of politicians. Ten people may all have different reasons for voting for the same candidate. One person may like their economic policies, while another values their experience. Certain voters might like their stance on health care, yet others simply respond to their personality. Voting records, public service, personal connections, and more—they are all factors that get considered when people decide who to vote for. In this particular case, the voters have all come together to elect the same person, but their reasons for doing so vary quite a bit. This is true whether we're trying to sell politicians, podcasts, or pizza.

Sound complicated? It's not. Your task—at least for right now—is to set yourself apart from the competitors, to find some way to differentiate yourself in an increasingly noisy market. You do that by being the most "you" you can be.

MINDSET SHIFT
Differentiation is about providing a compelling
answer to the following question: What
are the stories only you can tell?

No two people are exactly alike, and the same is true with restaurants. To stand out, you need to identify the things that set you apart from all the other brands out there. I've done this exercise with clients, listeners, students, colleagues, and friends, and what begins as a seemingly impossible task always—and I mean *always*—proves this theory to be true. Even two pizza places that share the same street corner will possess qualities that set them apart; you just have to learn how to identify them.

I can (and will) give a bunch of examples, but I'll start with my own story. I live here in New York City, where I work as a restaurant coach. I help restaurant owners build more profitable businesses. Since launching the company in 2016, I've worked with hundreds of restaurants to help them do exactly what I'm now asking you to do. In one of the most saturated markets in the world, I compete against (literally) hundreds of other coaches, consultants, and agencies. Why should someone hire me as opposed to one of my competitors? Don't for a second think that I haven't gotten that question a thousand times before. The answer, I've come to realize, lies in my *story*.

My perspective, experience, and unique set of skills are what set me apart from my competitors. For example, did you know I originally came to the city to pursue a career in the arts? Over the years I've spent time as an actor, writer, director, producer, photographer, and filmmaker. As I began my marketing career,

I realized I possessed a whole host of skills that other marketers simply did not have. That was a key differentiator. I realized I was something of a one-stop shop when it came to brand strategy and content creation.

I also bring a ton of operational experience to the table. When I first arrived in the city, I did what many starving artists do: I got a job waiting tables. But what began as a day job slowly turned into a passion. Day after day I was learning more about food and wine, and eventually that helped me get better jobs at better restaurants. I worked my way up from host to server to captain to maître d' to manager. From 2004 to 2012, I went through a string of nine different restaurant openings—most of them high-profile properties with big names at the helm. What seemed like a random stretch of stressful experiences has proven to be invaluable in my career as a restaurant coach.

I've kept my company small because it allows me to stay nimble. It also gives me the opportunity to be hands-on with my clients. When you hire *me*, you get *me*. I believe the best way to attract consumers is to create a product people need. No Facebook ad or landing page will fix a brand that's broken. Make a quality product that's both unique and delicious, and it becomes that much easier to attract and retain customers. So while there are bigger, fancier agencies out there, I am convinced that the best way to serve my clients is to get down into the mud and help them solve interesting problems.

Those are just a few of the stories that only I can tell. And though I keep adding to the list, I know I offer three key differentiators: First and foremost, it's my unique set of skills. Second, it's my operational experience. And finally, it's the size of my company. *Small* is a differentiation point for me. *Hands-on* is something that separates me from my competitors. Because of that, I can stay nimble and more readily share my *knowledge* directly with my clients.

What does all that have to do with you? I want you to adopt a similar mindset. Like we spoke about in Chapter 2, your product is not for everyone. Certainly there are limited customers for the services I provide, and the same is true with your business. As we move forward, I'm going to push you to get clear on exactly what kind of experience you offer and exactly who it's for. *What is the product? Who is it for? How can you reach them?* Identifying the qualities that set you apart from your competitors is crucial. If there is a secret sauce, differentiation is the key ingredient. Note, however, that it's not a magic salve you can simply apply to your business. Differentiation must be baked into the recipe. It takes focus and hard work. Again . . . *marketing of the thing can't make up for the thing.*

Upon first glance differentiation may seem counterintuitive—this idea that we should be turning away business—but I promise it's the only way to attract a passionate base of raving fans. To prove my point, I want to look at some big brands that have done this particularly well. Apple made waves in their early days for developing what's called a *closed* system. Starbucks has built an empire that attracts consumers who prefer the strong taste of their coffee to weaker-tasting alternatives. For years Volvo's unique, boxy design was synonymous with their dedication to safety. The best companies in the world know what they believe in, and they know who their products are for. That is true for car companies, consumer electronics brands, running shoes, coffee, amusement parks, beer, colleges, airlines, and yes . . . restaurants.

Whenever I begin working with a new client, I always ask them to do an exercise for me. It's the same exercise I'm going to ask you to complete at the end of this chapter. I invite them to define their restaurant through a series of stories. I ask, "What are the stories only you can tell?" And before they can protest, I give them an example. I walk them through the exercise, imagining that I was hired by Danny Meyer to help do the marketing for his beloved Gramercy Tavern. You don't have to be a New Yorker to know who Danny Meyer is; a quick Google search will show that he's one of the most successful restaurateurs on the planet. He's the owner of USHG, a restaurant group here in New York City that includes Union Square Cafe, Gramercy Tavern, The Modern, and more; he also happens to be the founder of a little fast-food chain you may have heard of called Shake Shack.

My wife and I love Gramercy Tavern; in fact, for years we were regulars. Every Sunday evening we would make the trip into the city, snag two seats at the corner of the bar, and enjoy a quiet dinner together. She was teaching full-time back then, and I was still managing restaurants. Sundays were our only day off together, and those dinners were one of our cherished weekly rituals. Because of that, I've gotten to know the company quite well. And these are a few of the stories that only they can tell:

- It's owned by famed restaurateur Danny Meyer.
- It's the restaurant that really launched the career of Chef Tom Colicchio, a man who would go on to create his own empire with Craft and become the host of the popular TV show *Top Chef.*
- The restaurant won the 2008 James Beard Award for Out-standing Restaurant.

- It's the only restaurant that's ever called 42 East 20th Street home.
- Their current chef is Michael Anthony, a James Beard Award winner himself.
- The restaurant is home to an original Stephen Hannock painting. This world-renowned artist has work hanging in some of the most prestigious museums on the planet including the Smithsonian and The Met.
- The restaurant has two separate dining rooms—a more casual tavern up front and a formal dining room in back.

Now I'm asking you to do the same for your restaurant. These stories will become the foundation for all the work you're going to do from here on out. By identifying these stories—the ones that only you can tell—you'll start to see yourself the way your customers see you. Remember, the first thing a consumer will typically do is compile a list of their options. If they want sushi, they're going to pull up the sushi category either in their minds or in the app on their phone. How do you stand out from the competitors? The answer lies in these stories.

A "story" can be just about anything—your menu, a specific dish, the chef, your managers, your wine program, a signature cocktail, the beer list, your logo, the lighting, the music, decor, your address, ownership, service staff, glassware, the steps of service, and so on. Anything you do that sets you apart from the other restaurants in your category is a tool you can use to help tell your story. This exercise is where you celebrate yourself and the business you've built. And yes, all of us have stories that only we can tell. Certainly we know that on a personal level; I'm now challenging you to embrace that in your business as well.

If you take only one thing away from this book, I hope it's this idea of differentiation. Surviving in a noisy marketplace is near impossible unless you find some way to stand out. I begged you in the early pages of the book (just as I did in the beginning of this chapter): we don't need *just another* anything. Be creative, be bold, be yourself. I promise you will find a community of passionate individuals who will be glad that they found you.

ASSIGNMENT #5

Your assignment here is very simple. I want you to write down at least ten stories that only you can tell. Extra credit if you identify more. In reality, you should be able to write down thirty or forty if you really try. But for now, ten will suffice. Again, simply answer the question: *"What are the stories only you can tell?"*

CHAPTER 6
ABCD LEADS TO E

I've dedicated Part One of this book to my five-step framework for marketing absolutely anything in the world. The ABCDs of Marketing is a way of simplifying the topic to help chefs, owners, and operators wrap their heads around this idea of how to position themselves in the market. How do you get started? Simply by going through those early exercises. Too often restaurant owners skip ahead to the part where they get to cook delicious food, but by now hopefully you see the importance of first answering the question: For whom are we making this delicious food?

Understanding who you're serving and how you're uniquely qualified to serve them requires a shift in the way you approach your work. Understanding who your competitors are and how you're different is the only way to stand out in a noisy marketplace. The ABCD exercise is the first thing I do with any new client, but there's one final step to the framework . . .

ABCD eventually leads to E, and E stands for *everything*. Every choice you make communicates something to your audience. The lighting, music, menu, and service style all say something to a prospective diner. The signage out front, whether you realize it or not, is cueing your guests for the type of experience they can expect. Your website says something about who you are, as does the pricing and presentation of your menu. As they get to know you, your guests are deciding—often subconsciously—whether this is somewhere they belong.

Moving forward, I want you to divide up your efforts into two distinct areas: internal marketing and external marketing. Traditionally, internal marketing is used to describe how a company communicates with its employees, but I give this a little spin when I speak about marketing restaurants. For our purposes, I want you to think of internal marketing as everything that happens within the four walls of your restaurant and external marketing as everything beyond.

Plenty of restaurant owners have built empires for themselves simply by following their gut, using intuition to make important decisions about their businesses. But for every success story, there are ten failures. I believe the only path to success is to be deliberate with the choices you make. There is a simple fact that's impossible to ignore in our line of work, and it's best summed up in the words of the inimitable Stephen Sondheim:

MINDSET SHIFT
God is in the details.[3]

When I tell people I'm a marketer, they usually start talking to me about social media or SEO tactics. They ask me about email marketing strategies and best practices when it comes to web design and app interface. And those are important aspects to how a business gets marketed, but they're neglecting one key piece of the equation: the experience itself. As I often say, marketing of the thing can't make up for the thing. The best way to market a product is to create a product so remarkable that it demands attention. To focus only on external efforts is to ignore one of the most powerful tools we have at our disposal—the meal itself.

If you know who you are and who you're for, then the next step is to figure out ways to communicate that. There are myriad ways to do that, but the best way to get started is to run a marketing audit. I want you to take an hour of your life to step back from daily operations to assess all your current efforts. Since we're going to divide things up into internal and external, why not start there?

An internal-marketing audit begins on the curb in front of your restaurant. I want you to look at the parking lot, the front door, and the signage advertising your restaurant. What sort of impression would a potential diner get if they knew nothing else about the restaurant? Walk inside and take note of the lighting, music, and decor. What would a first-time diner think? Sit down at one of the tables; in fact, sit at several different tables. Are the chairs comfortable? What are your guests looking at while they're dining? Look over the menu, paying careful attention to the layout and design. Is the menu easy to navigate, or is it confusing? What sort of font is used? How are things arranged? Are the descriptions appetizing? Does the cuisine fit with the rest of the room? Sit through a bit of service and watch the way your servers move through the space and engage with your customers. Are they executing the vision you have for the restaurant?

And what about those customers? Do they seem to be enjoying

themselves? What about when it comes time to pay? Do the prices match up with the experience your staff provided? What do you think a first-time diner will say about your restaurant when they talk to a coworker the next morning? What about a regular? Is there a level of consistency from table to table, visit to visit?

From there, move on to an external-marketing audit to assess all of your further efforts. Start with digital assets like your website and social media channels. These should be an extension of your brand. Does the imagery and text properly communicate the kind of dining experience you are crafting? Google the name of your restaurant and see what pops up. Do you rank first in a simple Google search? How does the listing look? If you're not first, who is? What would a prospective diner think about that? Scan through some of the review sites like Yelp, Google, Foursquare, and Tripadvisor. What sorts of ratings are you receiving? Are there consistent compliments? Any common criticisms? How else might a diner discover you—maybe through a reservation platform like Open-Table or Resy? Are you listed on sites like Eater, Michelin, Zagat, or Infatuation? Have you been reviewed by any notable publications? What is the overall impression a diner would get if they read a handful of those reviews? Finally, then, I want you to think about your owned channels like email, SMS, YouTube, and perhaps a blog. How often do you send out communications? How do they look? Is there a discernible strategy? Have you established a cohesive plan for attracting and retaining clients? Are your external marketing efforts in line with the kind of restaurant you've created?

The goal of these marketing audits is to get a realistic assessment of your current efforts. I want you to identify the things that are working and those that are not. I want you to make a wish list of sorts: the website needs better pictures, the captions on our social media posts need to be more expressive, the service style needs to be more relaxed, we need a new playlist during brunch, etc. Again, by going through the ABCD exercise, you should now have a better idea of who you are and who you're for. Your job now is to make sure that everything is in alignment. The presentation of the food must match the prices. The service style must match the vibe of the place. The website must capture and communicate what it's like to dine at the restaurant. The emails must inspire people to open them and click on the offers inside.

Details matter. Don't assume that people will immediately grasp what you're trying to do. You must communicate it over and over and over again. If you're a romantic fine-dining restaurant, then the dim lighting will help tell that story, as will the light jazz in the background. The high prices and small portions will communicate luxury to the diner, as will the elegant website and understated signage out front. I use this because it's an obvious example, but the same is true with every concept. Details matter, so be deliberate about each and every choice you make.

ASSIGNMENT #6

Just as I outlined throughout this chapter, I want you to conduct an internal- and external-marketing audit. Done properly, it shouldn't take more than an hour or so and will be an invaluable step in the process. Take two sheets of paper and label one "Internal" and the other "External." On the first sheet, I want you to assess all your internal-marketing efforts. Tell me about the music, lighting, decor, service style, pricing, menus, food quality, beverage options, presentation, and so on. The second sheet of paper is where you're going to collect all your thoughts about your external-marketing efforts. How does your website look? What do you think about your social media presence? Do you have an established email marketing plan? How are you using content strategy to engage with prospective diners? We're not fixing anything just yet. Right now I just want you to assess your current efforts to determine whether you're telling a cohesive story.

PART TWO
INTERNAL MARKETING

CHAPTER 7

IMAGINE THE ENDING

Over the course of this book, I'm introducing you to a series of mindset shifts—new ways of looking at familiar ideas. I'll remind you that the very first one said this: "We don't sell food; we sell experiences." If someone simply needs to eat, there are faster, cheaper, more efficient alternatives out there. Relatively speaking, dining out is expensive, both in terms of time and money. Dinner at a restaurant usually comes out of a family's entertainment budget, not their grocery budget. So we need to start thinking about it in terms of crafting a specific kind of experience for a specific kind of person. The food is certainly part of that experience but so is the service and the decor. All of it adds up to an experience, and that is what we are marketing when we market a restaurant. This begs two important questions: How do we begin to craft an experience, and how exactly do we market that experience?

You wouldn't get into your car unless you knew where you were headed, so why would you build a restaurant before you understood exactly what you were trying to create? This is where the early exercises come in handy. Hopefully by now you have a grasp on your market, and you understand where you might fit in. You have an audience in mind and understand how that audience needs to be served. Now you simply need to close your eyes and imagine a solution to their problems. Your restaurant should be the answer to someone's prayers. All you have to do is execute that vision.

This idea of working backward is something you should apply to every aspect of your business. If you want people to rave about their meal, then you need to give them something worth raving about. If you want to attract the kind of clientele willing to pay the high prices you need to charge, then you need to craft an experience they can't find anywhere else. If you want people to come back again and again, you've got to give them a specific reason to return.

As an owner I know it's easy to spend all your time putting out fires, running from one emergency to the next. The bartender no-showed, the seafood delivery never came in, table thirty-two found a hair in their food, and on and on. It's easy to get lost in the daily chaos of running a restaurant; you often spend so much time working *in* your business that you don't have enough time to work *on* your business.

So how do you break the cycle and take a more deliberate approach to the work? As the saying goes, "The first step is admitting you have a problem." We can't do any of the great work that's ahead of us until we carve out the time and brain space to devote to it. How can you pull yourself out of the daily grind to be able to work in a more productive direction? I can't answer that for you; all I can tell you is that it must be done.

In the last chapter, I invited you to do a marketing audit on your business. Hopefully you took the time to assess your current and past efforts. When we talk about internal marketing, we're talking about the actual experience of dining at your restaurant, and environment plays a big role in how a guest thinks about the experience. Before we even set foot in the restaurant, the diner is looking at our signage and front windows. Once inside, they're taking in the music, lighting, and decor. They're inspecting the silver and glassware. They're surveying the menus—reading the descriptions and taking note of the prices. They're looking at the presentation and tasting everything they put in their mouths. The service affects their experience, as do the temperature and tone of the room. Why, then, do so many brands focus on social media before they take the time to solidify the actual dining experience?

Just like we did with the marketing audit, I want you to start out in front of your restaurant and think about how a diner would feel arriving at your front door. What is the experience you're trying to create, and do the building, parking lot, and signage help communicate that? What needs to change to convey the right message to a prospective diner? Look over the list you made during the audit and identify just three things you can fix immediately. Do whatever you need to do to rectify those issues.

Now it's time to head inside. Environment plays a big role in how a diner experiences their meal. Is the lighting too bright, too dim, or just right? Does the volume of the music feel right for the space? What about the type of music being played? What's the feeling you get when you survey the dining room? Does the decor support what you're trying to do? Look over the lighting fixtures, wall coverings, tables, and chairs. What would you think walking in here for the first time? And what about the layout? Are the tables spaced too far apart? Are they too close? Does the noise from the bar spill over into the dining room? Is that okay? If not, how could you fix it? Glance at the list you made during your audit. What are three things you can fix this week? Take care of them and then figure out what three things you'll tackle next.

Sit down for a meal. Or, better yet, sit in the corner and watch other people enjoy a meal. Watch carefully when a party gets seated at a table. Where do they look? How long does it take for them to get comfortable? Pay attention to the way they engage with the service staff. Does it look like they want more attention or less? How do they navigate the menu? What dishes seem to grab their attention? What do they comment about, complain about? How much time passes until they get their drinks, their appetizers, their entrées? Does it look like they're enjoying themselves? Is there something you could do to make them more comfortable? Write down your ideas. What about the environment might help them settle into the meal? Perhaps it's the layout of the menu or the way the server explains the menu? Maybe the music is too loud . . . or too quiet. Maybe they need something to look at. A high-end restaurant might need some art on the walls or more interesting design flourishes; a more casual restaurant might benefit from some TVs. What sorts of changes could you make to put these diners at ease? Again, use the notes you took during the audit as a guide. If possible, identify three easy items to fix and take care of them this week.

The dining experience is housed within a physical space, and so you need to take that into account when creating a restaurant.

On the one hand, I know this can feel overwhelming. But viewed another way, let this empower you. There are hundreds of little details that go into making a restaurant, and you have the power to change anything that isn't working. As I said earlier, the first step is to acknowledge the problem, to say to yourself, "This can be better." The next step is simply putting a plan into place.

ASSIGNMENT #7

What I'm getting you to do here is identify problems, prioritize those problems, then fix those problems. In reality, that's what you're going to do from here on out. Turning a business around requires us to get good at problem-solving; that's so much of the work I do as a restaurant coach. Today, I want you to look over the notes from your audit—specifically from your internal-marketing audit—and find the low-hanging fruit. What are the nine or ten things you could fix this week? Make a list, then start crossing things off one at a time.

CHAPTER 8

AMBASSADORS AND EVANGELISTS

I assume that if you've gone to the effort of starting your own business that you're passionate about what you do—about the people you serve and the service you provide. If you've started to apply some of the earlier lessons in this book, hopefully you've woven some of that into the day-to-day of your restaurant. The problem, though, is this: the interactions you have with your employees and guests are limited. While most of us wish we could be in all places at once, we also know that it's an impossible task.

You can't be there to explain the menu to every single guest, nor can you moderate every conversation those guests have when they tell their friends and family about the meal they had at your restaurant. Shaping a brand's image is a challenge for all marketers—and has been for centuries—but now technology has made that even harder. Why? Because most of our marketing is now happening without us. Word of mouth is now done online, where opinions can spread faster than wildfire.

MINDSET SHIFT
80 percent of your marketing is
happening behind your back.

There are only so many people who will care enough to open your emails, only so many people who will see your most recent social media post, only so many people who you'll reach with your new lunch promotion. The rest is a result of word of mouth. And in the age of technology, the biggest question becomes: What are all those people going to say about you?

Your staff is responsible for delivering the message to your customers, and your customers are then the ones spreading that message far and wide. Together they will have a huge impact on your bottom line, and so you need to build a strategy that accounts for that. I lovingly call these two groups Ambassadors and Evangelists.

AMBASSADORS

Imagine you're stuck on a life raft with a handful of your employees, idly floating out in the middle of a huge lake. You can see the shoreline in all directions and have identified at least half a dozen docks that would provide safe harbor. The question is: Which way do you row? Without guidance your employees will start rowing in different directions, ensuring that the boat pretty much stays right where it is. Instead, you need to help guide the team. A great leader sets a goal, pointing to the shore with confidence: "There! That's where we're going." It's been said that strong leadership is about getting your team to all row in the same direction.

The analogy is simple, and the work we've done in the early part of the book should provide some of the tools needed for you to set a course for your staff. That's the foundational work we did in Part One. Now you must transfer that information to your team because the reality is you're not the one rowing. You're simply standing there, pointing to the shore, telling them when to dip their oars in the water. True leadership is a rare quality these days but absolutely crucial for building a successful business. So how do you do it, then? How do you get everyone rowing in the same direction? In my experience great leadership comes down to these four things:

1. **Articulating a clear vision**
2. **Finding the right people who can execute your vision**
3. **Establishing clear expectations for the team**
4. **Creating a culture that promotes your core values**

It's not enough just to hire qualified people and throw them into a station. You must find the right people for what you're looking to do, and you need a systematic way for bringing them along on the journey. While it may be *your* vision, you entrust a small group of people to execute that vision. In a sense we're talking about hiring, training, and managing—but it goes deeper than that. If you'll allow, I'd like to introduce you to a new way of thinking about staffing your restaurant.

1) ARTICULATING A CLEAR VISION

In his book *Start with Why,* Simon Sinek outlines something he calls the Golden Circle.[4] Most organizations don't understand why they do what they do. The best companies, however, take an inside-out approach, letting their "why" dictate how they operate and what kinds of products and services they provide.

To me, his is the most articulate definition for how leaders provide vision for a company, but I'm going to take it one step further. Last year I gave a presentation with my friend and colleague Shawn Walchef (founder of Cali BBQ Media), where we invited the audience to consider their "two whys." These are two questions that changed his business—two questions that hold the key to connecting with not only your patrons but your staff as well.

1.   Why did you start your business?
2.   Why does that matter?

Answer those, and you'll be miles ahead of your competitors. Shawn is certainly a testament to that.

For the husband and wife who run the cozy little breakfast spot in town, it can be something as simple as "we want to support our community by using fresh ingredients from local farmers to create delicious food for the people who live here." The pizza place that just opened may simply want "to bring authentic Neapolitan-style pizza to the neighborhood." The cool, new gastropub in town exists "to celebrate the incredible accomplishments and variety of American craft brewers."

Vision comes in all forms, but it must be identified for it to be articulated. Your answers to those two questions will define everything else you do—who you hire and how you train them, the ingredients you source and how they're prepared, the prices you charge and the kind of patrons you attract. Once you understand why you do what you do, stick it on the wall (literally if you must) and point to it whenever someone needs to be reminded. Why should anyone care about what we do? That's why!

2) FINDING THE RIGHT PEOPLE WHO CAN EXECUTE YOUR VISION

Now you've got some clarity. You know why you exist, how your approach differs from others, and exactly what kind of experience you provide for your customers. But you need buy-in from the people who will be on the front lines. For most of your patrons, the reservationist who answers the phone will be their first point of contact. The busboys you hire will have more contact with your guests in a week than you possibly could in a year. The line cooks who are charged with preparing the food each night will have a greater impact on a guest's experience than the award-winning chef you hired to oversee the kitchen.

So how do you find the right people? It begins by defining the qualities you want to cultivate in your team. Do you want nice novices or polished professionals? Do you value education over experience? If so, what sort of knowledge is required to excel at your restaurant? How much weight do you put on a résumé? There are no wrong answers—and certainly the approach will be different for every restaurant—but to find it, you have to first know what you're looking for.

To begin, I want you to write your manifesto. In many ways this is an extension of the work you did in Chapter 5. What types of people are you looking for? What are the things they must have when they walk in the door, and what are the things they'll learn over time? Do that for each and every department, each position if you must. Again, until you know what you're looking for, you'll never be able to find it.

But once you do know what you're looking for, it becomes easier to figure out how to go get it. For example, if you want your servers to have a certain level of food and beverage knowledge, then maybe the first step in the hiring process is a simple test to see how the candidates stack up against each other. If personality is key to your establishment, then you need to figure out what kinds of questions to ask in an interview that will help reveal personality. If you want cooks who are eager to learn, then you need to use the interview process to teach them something. That will allow you to see how they internalize the information you give and put it into practice. All this obviously takes planning, but not as much as you might think. And I assure you it's better than the alternative. In fact, I'm guessing many of you are already familiar with the alternative.

Stop doing interviews the way everyone else does interviews. Worry less about their recent experience, and work hard to see what they learned from that experience. Spend less time talking about the past, and put more focus on the future. Your place is unique, and the things you're looking for should be specific. Use the hiring process as a way of finding the right people. With just a little planning, you'll be able to attract better candidates and get them to buy in to what you're building.

3) ESTABLISHING CLEAR
EXPECTATIONS FOR THE TEAM

Once you've identified the right people, you need to put a system in place that will bring them up to speed quickly. Of course, we're talking about training, and I'm going to invite you to rethink your process ever so slightly. Most operators I know set a five-to-seven-day training period, but what happens if you extend your time horizon to ninety days? No one will learn everything in a week, so simply acknowledge that from the start. Now the question becomes: How can you bring this new hire along so that ninety days down the road, they are every bit as capable as your most seasoned employees?

That simple shift will change the relationship you build with new staff members and give you some runway to work with. Next, figure out what people need to know by the end of their first training shift. What about after their second, third, and fourth? How will you pass that knowledge along to them, and what are the systems you can put into place to ensure that they're learning what you need them to learn? How will you judge whether a new hire is ready to "go live"? And, most importantly, how will you continue to nurture their development in the weeks that follow? Everything should be aligned to get them to where they need to be by the end of their first ninety days. And, of course, if you're organized you can easily outline your expectations to these new employees: "We will expect you to know the following information by this date. We are going to track your progress in the following ways, with the expectation that ninety days from now you will be able to do x, y, and z." Really, it comes down to setting clear expectations for your team. Do it, and you'll find a whole new energy in your restaurant.

4) CREATING A CULTURE THAT PROMOTES YOUR CORE VALUES

Of course, that begs the question: What are your restaurant's core values? What would your employees tell me if I went and asked them? Food culture in America has exploded since the midnineties, and it's now a sought-after career path for millions of people. The low barrier of entry means just about anyone can get their foot in the door, but no two restaurants are exactly alike. This is as good a time as any to answer the following question: What do you stand for?

You've already started learning how to market your restaurant to consumers, but now I'm going to ask you to market your restaurant to potential staff members. What kinds of people might love to work at your restaurant? What sorts of opportunities can you provide for them? Who else are you competing with for those employees? How can you separate yourself from those competitors? Notice, I just applied the ABCD framework to illustrate how you can attract and retain the staff you need.

People want to work for companies that compensate them appropriately but also ones that acknowledge their contributions. Vision and values go hand in hand, and I believe they hold the key to creating a great work environment. Words matter. And so do your actions. Your people are listening and watching—and following your lead. Be the kind of person who leads by example. Show them how they should engage with your guests.

EVANGELISTS

The other side of this equation are those guests. The two hundred people you fed last night in your restaurant probably each told four of their friends this morning about their dining experience. The question is: What did they say? A great deal of focus should be put into giving your guests something to talk about. Unlike a new pair of shoes or a watch, they can't easily show off the experience they had the night before. Since word of mouth is so powerful, your job is to help them do it more effectively. Realize that the following conversation takes place millions of times a day, week after week, in countries all around the world:

> Your guest: "Last night we went to Restaurant X for dinner."
> Their friend: "Oh yeah? How was it?"
> Your guest: "Pretty good."
> Their friend: "Cool."

The conversation ends, and Restaurant X goes bankrupt some short time later. Why? Because "pretty good" doesn't cut it anymore; certainly it won't get people excited enough to go out of their way to book a reservation. As I mentioned earlier, you've got to give them a *reason to believe* . . .

Your guests are going to talk about you; we simply want to control the narrative. You want to get people so excited about their meal that they can't help but rave about it to their friends. This process starts by understanding what makes you unique. Remember we did an exercise back in Chapter 5 that started with the question: "What are the stories only you can tell?" The thing that makes you unique is also the thing that will make you memorable. That can be the beautiful chandelier in your front foyer, the wall of self-serve beer taps by the bar, the dramatic presentation of your Ribeye for Two, or the unique way you serve your martinis.

Mostly I find that restaurants do things just like all the other restaurants do things. There is a sameness to most experiences, and people forget which one's which. But people want to be entertained and inspired. In fact, they want to be wowed! And you'd be surprised how little it takes sometimes to impress people. If your restaurant were a religion, then your patrons should be your congregation. How does a religion grow? The same way a restaurant does. You want people to show up week after week to hear your sermon and then be so moved that they can't help but go share their experience. This is the very definition of evangelism.

Find opportunities to surprise and delight your guests! This is why it's so important to know your market. You should understand what your competitors are doing so that you can create separation. The only chance you have at standing out in a noisy marketplace is to create a unique experience. Play with the way you present your menu or plate your dishes. Create drama as a means of capturing attention. A dish that gets people to ooh and ahh will also be the kind of dish that gets photographed and shared on social media. It will get talked about and remembered and ordered over and over again as new guests try to recapture the experience they saw online.

Give your patrons a shorthand they can use to talk about you, and create opportunities for them to go share your story. In today's internet age, it's the only way to stay relevant. It's also the only way to survive. In the end, you need to find ways to create Ambassadors for your brand and Evangelists to go spread the good word.

ASSIGNMENT #8

Marketing textbooks often talk about something called a value proposition, meaning what is it that makes a diner choose you over one of your competitors? This is very similar to differentiation, but on a single sheet of paper I want you to write down five to ten things that make you a more compelling choice than the competition. Next to each one, I want you to tell me exactly why it made the list, and then I want you to explain what about the dining experience hammers home that point. If you have trouble with any of this, then you're starting to get an idea about where you need to put your focus moving forward.

CHAPTER 9

TRANSACTIONS, VALUE, AND PRICE

I began this book by agreeing on a definition for marketing, and I'm going to do a similar thing here by inviting us all to define another key concept. What is a transaction? The *Oxford English Dictionary* offers the following definition:

> **trans·ac·tion:** /tranˈzakSH(ə)n/ - *noun.*
> An instance of buying or selling something;
> an exchange between two entities; a business deal.[5]

For our purposes I want us to focus on that second part of the definition and expand it just a bit. *A transaction is an exchange between two entities, where both sides give and receive something.* As it turns out, this is a somewhat important revelation. As business owners, we make a trade with our customers. In a way we're now starting to talk about price, though the number listed on the menu isn't all that's exchanged. Confused? Don't be.

When we list halibut on our menu, we are selling so much more than just a well-cooked piece of fish. We are selling the chef's expertise and creativity, their years of training and experience. And of course we are also selling the experience of enjoying that halibut in our beautiful dining room. So yes, we are selling a filet of halibut, but we're also trading away so much more. If you ever think to yourself, "Maybe our prices are too high," I want you to go back and make sure you've done the full calculation.

Likewise, on the other side of the transaction, the diner is also giving up more than just the thirty-two dollars listed on the menu. What am I talking about?

> **MINDSET SHIFT**
> In addition to their hard-earned cash, our patrons pay us with the three most precious resources they have: time, attention, and trust.

We thus have a responsibility to honor their side of the transaction by bringing as much of ourselves as we can to each interaction. This, of course, speaks to the idea of empathy, something found at the heart of all great marketing. What is empathy? It's the ability to see the world through another person's eyes. It takes an incredible amount of humility and generosity to do that well, and especially for those of us in the service industry, I think it's a quality worth cultivating. Let me show you how this works in practice.

Married couples celebrate their anniversary just once a year, and I can speak from my own experience—especially when our son was very young—that night was often the one nice meal we enjoyed all year. For several years dining out became a luxury for us; it was a cost my wife and I couldn't justify more than once or twice a year. The decision about which reservation to keep was fraught. When any of those meals started going south—as one did just a couple years back—all we could think of were the other restaurants that had been on our list. Each bite seemed to be filled with regret. We couldn't help feeling that we'd made the wrong decision. Aside from the couple hundred bucks that got flushed down the toilet, we had also squandered our one date night of the year.

As restaurant professionals it's sometimes impossible to know what's going on with a given table. Did any of the staff know the importance this meal held for us? No. Could they have made the effort to learn? Absolutely. But by the time we got to entrées, it was obvious that the restaurant was not living up to all the accolades it had received. The service was not attentive enough for the prices they were charging and the food wasn't as dynamic as the reviewers had led us to believe. Was it the end of the world? Certainly not. But it was disappointing, and you better believe that we told this story often to friends, family, and colleagues when they asked us about the restaurant.

By the end of this chapter, there are three realizations I want you to come to. The first is what we just discussed—that both parties exchange something during any transaction, and often there are unlisted items being exchanged (like time, attention, and trust). The second shift I want you to make is this: Unlike just about every other industry in the world where the transaction lasts just a few minutes (or a few seconds), a transaction in our world can last hours. Literally hours! Your diners sit down with the understanding that the server is going to try to sell things to them for the next two hours.

You not only have so many opportunities to sell, but you also have so many opportunities to ensure your guests have a phenomenal time. Other industries would die for the kind of contact we have with our customers, and yet most of us squander it night after night.

Instead, what if you used those two hours to get to know your guests, to engage with them and exceed their expectations? There are ways to both provide better service and increase the guest check average. (And no, those two things are not at odds with each other.) The dining experience is the transaction, and people come to us to be wowed. So what exactly are you doing to honor your end of the deal? Sadly, instead of celebrating this, the industry we work in prefers that we talk about cover counts and table turn times. We focus on the numbers as if quantity can make up for diminished quality. If that approach worked for previous generations, I'm here to tell you that it's not going to work moving forward.

Finally, then, there's one more shift I want you to make, and it has to do with a word we all tend to overuse: value. First, the formal definition:

value: /ˈvalyoo/ - *noun.*
the regard that something is held to deserve;
the importance, worth, or usefulness of something.[6]

Viewing transactions through this lens of *value* makes it impossible not to take into account the other side. You charge more for a dish than it cost you to make. That's how you turn a profit. And the diner chooses to book a reservation because they see the *value* in what you're offering. Dinner at your restaurant is useful to them; it has worth. Which makes sense, right? You are, after all, saving them from prepping the meal and cleaning up afterward; you're also offering a dining room that (we'll assume) is nicer than their kitchen at home. The consumer looks at the prices on your menu and thinks, "This experience is worth more to me than the price they're charging." The final shift? Transactions work when both sides win.

So to determine a price for the thing you're selling, you first need to figure out what that thing is worth to the person we're seeking to serve. To do this sort of calculation, you must see the world as your customers see it, think about the meal as they will experience it. What will they be expecting, and what might they think afterward? Is the experience you're crafting worth what you're charging? Should you charge less? Could you charge more? So how about a better definition for a word we all tend to overuse? I've never been great at math, but even I can get behind a formula like this.

MINDSET SHIFT
Worth minus price equals value.

Your job as a business owner is to make sure that equation stays balanced. That's how you get people to come try you out, to choose you over a competitor, and to return for a meal time and time again. When they see the value in the experience, they will rave about it to friends and keep you top of mind for future meals. You beat out your competitors by communicating value again and again, by highlighting the things that set you apart, illuminating all the reasons why you're better. Do that creatively and consistently, and you will have built not just a successful marketing strategy but a successful business as well.

ASSIGNMENT #9

On a single sheet of paper, I want you to describe all that you're giving away on your end of the transaction. Besides a well-cooked dish, what else are you trading away? The deeper you go, the more useful this exercise becomes.

CHAPTER 10

MENU MAGIC

The people in your dining room are all here for different reasons. Some are celebrating birthdays or graduations, while others may be closing important business deals. You've got a couple at the bar grabbing a quick bite before their movie, a business deal closing in the corner, and a family of four just trying to have a civilized meal before heading home for the night. Despite those differences, there is still one thing they all have in common: each and every one of them will be handed the same document—your menu.

> **MINDSET SHIFT**
> Your menu is the most valuable piece
> of real estate in your restaurant.

When designed properly your menu can speed up turn times, save on waste, drive more revenue, and improve the quality of service in your restaurant. As you're probably realizing, it can also work against you in all four of those areas. To make sure that doesn't happen, I'm going to invite you to take a closer look at how you're utilizing this key asset.

This may seem overly obvious, but we are in the age of big data. These days we can measure just about every aspect of an operation, but none of it is any good unless we take the time to analyze the numbers and make the appropriate changes. This, in a nutshell, is what menu engineering is all about. Much has been written on the subject, so I won't waste the space here. I'll simply say that you need to know your numbers inside and out. Specifically, you need to understand the profitability and popularity of the dishes you serve. That will help you guide the diner toward the kind of experience you want them to have.

To do that you need a plan. While many establishments are now starting to incorporate table ordering and kiosks (solutions I wholeheartedly support), I'm going to focus primarily on how we can maximize our good, old-fashioned paper menus. Having done this for a while, there are a handful of insights I'd like to pass along regarding menu design and the idiosyncrasies of human behavior.

TEN INSIGHTS FOR BETTER MENU DESIGN

1. This is not always true, but very often the first and last item in a given category will sell more than items in the middle of the pack. This is worth keeping in mind as you decide how to list the items on your menu. For example, if I'm laying out my dessert menu, and I know the chocolate mousse is my biggest seller, I might decide to bury that in

the middle of the pack rather than put it right at the top. Instead, perhaps I'll list another—more profitable—item (like a crème brûlée) first, in an effort to guide consumer behavior. Likewise, if I find that most tables typically order just a single dessert to share at the end of the meal, I might decide to create a special dessert for two—like an apple tart—and list that near the bottom. Again, since the first and last items typically sell more than those listed in between, this would be a good strategy for either driving more revenue (in the case of the dessert for two) or more profit (in the case of the crème brûlée).

2. English is read left to right, top to bottom, so the eye naturally starts in the top left corner of the menu, zips over to the top right corner, before landing somewhere in the middle of the page. Those three areas are your most valuable real estate. (By contrast, operators in Israel—where Hebrew is read right to left—would simply reverse the order.) It sounds counterintuitive, but diners don't read a menu the same way they would read a book. They are not thorough, at least not in the beginning. By understanding that we can arrange our menus in a way that will help guide the diner. Perhaps a big callout in the upper left corner or a box featuring some of your signatures right smack in the middle?

3. Less is more; embrace the white space. A menu shouldn't just be a list of all the dishes the chef is prepared to make. Instead it should be focused—a curated list that's easy for the diner to consider. If you find yourself decreasing the

font size just to fit all the items on the page, you should stop and reconsider. The more items you have on your menu, the longer it takes your guests to decide. By streamlining the menu, we can trim valuable minutes off the table turn time. Quicker mealtimes equate to more covers. Plan accordingly.

4. Callouts are a great way to draw the diner's attention to where you want them to go. Undoubtedly, you've seen these on menus; hell, you're probably using some of these already. Still, here are some ideas worth considering: Try putting boxes around certain items, especially popular and/ or high-profit items. Include graphics or icons throughout the menu. I find this useful when calling out signatures and vegetarian options. The people who are looking for these items will find them more easily, and it'll ultimately cut down the amount of time the server spends at the table. As an added bonus, it'll also show your diners that you are attuned to their needs. Finally, don't forget about pictures. Most of the restaurants I work with use simple paper menus so they can make changes more easily, but if your menu is fairly set, you might want to look into a more durable laminated menu. If you're taking this route, you may want to double down by including some mouth-watering images of fan favorites.

5. A premium offering works in two key ways: First, simply by offering it you will get sales, which not only increases your guest check average but also helps you identify big spenders. Second, its existence will make other items seem much more reasonably priced. Listing a "premium" cut on

your menu for $85, for example, suddenly makes the $65 "regular" steak seem much more approachable. You can apply this strategy to almost every category on your menu. If your specialty cocktails are all priced at $12, why not offer something special for a few bucks more? List a bottle of cabernet for $350, and suddenly the $100 offering no longer seems so crazy. I promise this will make you more money and create a better experience for those guests who are willing to spend more money with you.

6. Consider listing cocktails or wines by the glass on the first page of your menu. It is, after all, the first thing you want people to order, so why not make that obvious? When the guests sit down and start thumbing through the menu, the drinks page will inevitably be the first thing they see. You can fortify this by training your servers to call it out on first approach: "I'll be back in just a second to walk you through the menu, but have you had a chance to look at the cocktails on the first page? What can I get for everyone?"

7. Sometimes it's best to pull a signature item from the menu altogether. This gives your servers something to talk about, all while creating a bit of scarcity in the eyes of the consumer. I've done this for multiple concepts, and on many occasions that "unlisted" item rises to the top of the product mix within a matter of weeks. It sounds counterintuitive I know, but it works. This is especially helpful for items that you know are good but just haven't caught on yet. Pull them from the menu and let your people do the work.

8. Assume that everyone coming in for dinner will order an appetizer and an entrée. The server's job, then, is to find ways to get them to order something else beyond what they were expecting to consume. Can you add a "Snacks" section to the menu so that diners can order something to nibble on while they review the menu. Do you offer side dishes for the table? Can you get people excited about dessert before they've even had their entrée course? Don't you remember how French restaurants used to sell soufflé back in the eighties? You can apply the same philosophy in your own restaurant today. Again, the strategy is to get them to order something they weren't expecting to order when they walked in the door. By introducing them to new items and guiding them through the experience, your servers and bartenders will drive more revenue, make better tips, and also create a better guest experience.

9. Does your menu provide opportunities for the servers to upsell? If a guest orders the Greek salad, the server should be able to ask if they want grilled chicken or shrimp added to that. If two people order the same wine, the server should immediately point out that there are four glasses to a bottle and there's a discount when ordering the full bottle. If someone orders a vodka martini, the server should know to recommend some of the premium spirits you carry. Likewise, if someone orders a steak, the server should know that red wine is a perfect pairing. Make sure there are opportunities throughout the menu for the server to upsell.

10. Psychology is a big factor when it comes to pricing, so I recommend scrapping the dollar sign (or euro, pound, etc.), the decimal point, and everything that would come after the decimal point. The only time humans ever come across two decimal places and a dollar sign is when they're considering cost. When possible, it's better not to remind people that they are in fact transacting. Instead of $9.99, simply list it as 10. Though, come to think of it, if you're going to charge 10 for something, you might as well just charge 12. Going from single digits to double digits is a big jump in the eyes of the consumer, but once you're already there you might as well get your money's worth. Literally!

ASSIGNMENT #10

Review your menu and see if you can apply any of the ten insights outlined in this chapter. No need to change everything all at once. To start, just identify some low-hanging fruit. Map out which changes will happen first, and then set a plan for bringing every-thing up to the level where you want it. There is a broader lesson here about patience. Breathe . . .

CHAPTER 11
STORYSELLING

Remember back to that interview we were discussing earlier. The interviewer looks up from the résumé in their hand and asks the candidate sitting across the table, "So can you tell me a little bit about yourself?" And never do they hear the response, "Well, I'm 5'9" and about 180 pounds with blue eyes and brown hair." True, the candidate gave them what they asked for, but no interviewer is interested in a recitation of facts and figures. What they want is a good story.

The same is true when it comes to online dating, professional sports, college admissions, and, yes, business. For millions of years, stories have been the foundation for all human connection. And yet for most of us, stories are something we take for granted—like a fish in water never realizing that it is, in fact, surrounded by water. But humans use stories in the most interesting ways, not the least of which is to sell. As it turns out, there's a word for that—it's called *storyselling*. I've spent the last two decades working in this industry and have identified five ways that chefs, owners, and operators often use stories to sell.

1) STORIES THAT COMMUNICATE A BRAND'S MISSION

We've spent a great deal of time covering this already, but your mission is something that must be communicated to a prospective diner. Why do you exist? What are you all about? How do you want people to think about your brand? If you open a high-end steakhouse, you will need to identify specific ways to communicate your mission to the diners you wish to serve. Just saying, "We're committed to serving premium cuts of beef" may not be enough. You will want to find ways to *prove* that to your audience. Imagine this conversation:

> Guest: "What's so special about this steakhouse?"
> You: "We serve the best steaks in town."
> Guest: "I like that other steakhouse just fine, thank you."

Without specifics, the conversation ends there. The diner wants to be convinced—they need a *reason to believe*—and without it there's little hope of getting them to give your restaurant a try. But if you truly are committed to serving the best steaks in town, then you need to find ways to tell that story. Imagine replaying this conversation in a more productive way:

> Guest: "What's so special about this steakhouse?"
> You: "We're committed to serving the best steaks in town."
> Guest: "And what makes your steaks so much better than those from the place across the street?"
> You: "We're sourcing the best meat available from places like Niman Ranch, and dry aging everything in house to guarantee quality."

Now just a couple of sentences into this conversation, and you're already starting to give some specifics. The earlier conversation was vague and relied on words like "*better*." But Niman Ranch means something. In fact, let me tell you a story.

Niman Ranch was founded in the early seventies by a guy named Bill Niman.[7] Based out of the San Francisco Bay Area, it's a network of hundreds of ranchers all over the American West who have committed themselves to a strict series of protocols and guidelines. Steak lovers know that Niman Ranch stands for quality. By aligning your restaurant with an organization like that, you're telling a story about who you are and why you exist. The same is true with dry aging your own steaks. It's a delicate process that's both costly and time-consuming. The sheer fact that you're committed to such an undertaking speaks volumes about the kind of steakhouse you are opening. Niman Ranch has a powerful origin story, and by aligning yourself with that organization, you help illustrate your mission.

2) STORIES THAT SPARK CONVERSATION

The Four Seasons restaurant was an institution for decades here in New York City. Situated on the ground floor of the Seagram Building in the heart of Midtown Manhattan, it was a place to see and be seen. At lunchtime, the tables were often filled with bestselling authors and their publicists, famous news anchors, big league sluggers, and Oscar-winning actresses. The crowd was serious about their overpriced food. And yet every meal ended with a jar of bright pink, homespun, gourmet cotton candy—a bit of fun amid all that severity. More than anything, it became a conversation piece for diners.

The huge portions at Carmine's in Times Square, the wide variety of sauces at Buffalo Wild Wings, and the over-the-top service at The French Laundry, all of these are things that people talk about long after they've left those restaurants. And since word of mouth is still the most powerful marketing tool we have, the question becomes: How can you use stories to extend the conversation beyond the four walls of your establishment?

3) STORIES THAT VALIDATE PRICE

When it comes to selling wine, there's a simple fact that many of us hesitate to admit: on a page listing fifty different bottles of Napa cabernet, there are far more similarities between them than there are differences. To a certain degree, everything on that page is a full-bodied red wine from California, so why is there such a discrepancy in price? This is what a guest will ask, and, of course, oftentimes the answer is simply that the winery has done a great job marketing their product. The consumer knows the label, recognizes the label, and is willing to pay a premium for that label. But I've found that to be an unsatisfying answer to give a guest. Instead, the best sommeliers learn how to tell stories about the wine.

Stories can do a lot to validate price in the eyes of the consumer. When we talk about winemaking regions, we're really telling a story about the people and the terroir of a given place. When we talk about the winemaker's approach, we're telling a story about style and pedigree. The method a winemaker uses is really a story about the craft of turning ordinary grapes into extraordinary wines. We can talk about the nature of a given vintage, the meaning of the wine's name, or even the story behind the picture on the label. At the end of the day, a mediocre wine with a good story gets sold more than a superior wine with no story.

Now apply that lesson to the rest of your menu—hell, to the rest of your business! Why should I get the premium cut instead of the regular steak? Why should I get the older vintage instead of the new one? Why should I dine at your restaurant when I can go to the place down the street for half the price? Tell a story that explains why your restaurant is worth the higher price tag—and make them believe it—and people will keep coming back to you.

4) STORIES THAT BRING A DEEPER APPRECIATION FOR THE PRODUCT

In the spring of 2005, Chef Grant Achatz opened Alinea, which has arguably become one of the most important restaurants in the world. It is the recipient of a coveted three Michelin Star rating and remains a mecca for foodies from all over the world. Yet the thing that brought the restaurant fame actually has very little to do with what's on the plate.

In 2007, just two years after he opened his prized dining room, Chef Achatz was diagnosed with Stage 4 tongue cancer. There was a very real possibility that one of the most celebrated chefs on the planet was going to lose his ability to taste his own food. In the end, the medical team at the University of Chicago was able to save his tongue (and his life) using an aggressive treatment of chemotherapy and radiation.[8]

Dinner at Alinea is an event full of unique quirks and theatrical surprises, and the story of the chef's battle with cancer gives the diner a deeper appreciation for the entire experience. When you know the story, it helps you understand the dichotomy of his cuisine—equal parts serious and whimsical. He was given a new lease on life and suddenly the idea of *carpe diem* became the seasoning to all his food. Dinner at Alinea is an event; it's about creating a unique, shared experience between guests. It is both heightened and theatrical. If Alinea is like no other restaurant in the world, it's because their story is all their own.

5) STORIES AS MYTHOLOGY

The Paris Wine Tasting of 1976—often referred to as "The Judgement of Paris"—was a famous blind tasting where a panel of eminent French judges swirled and sipped some of the most fabled wines in the world. For the whites, they tasted bottles from some of the most illustrious producers of Burgundy, as well as a sampling from a few upstart California chardonnays. By the end of the day, the audience (and judges) were shocked to discover that the 1973 Chateau Montelena Chardonnay had been crowned as the finest white wine in the world. That's right—a California wine beat out some of the most famous French producers![9]

The winemaker was a Croatian immigrant named Mike Grgich, who, over the course of twenty years, had worked his way up through Napa's most revered wineries. He was skilled, but at the time of the tasting, he was still a virtual unknown on the global stage. All that would quickly change once news got out about the Paris Wine Tasting. Within weeks, he was approached about starting his own wine label, and by the following spring, they were breaking ground and planting a slew of fresh vines.

Grgich Hills Estate now produces some of the finest wines in California, a full lineup that includes cabernet sauvignon, merlot, zinfandel, and, of course, chardonnay. Their origin story is a powerful bit of mythology that provides the foundation for everything they do. It gives the consumer a sense of scope, a way to contextualize what it is that makes the product so special. And you better believe that's helped them sell more wine!

————

Stories help anchor ideas in the mind of the consumer. You can use them to help your guests understand and appreciate what it is they're buying. You can also use them as a means of sharing your passion and knowledge with your customers. Stories help deepen the relationship between people—especially between buyer and seller—which is both good for business and a useful tool for building community. Remember that most of your marketing will happen behind your back by the people who work for you and the people who buy from you. Best to give some care to the way your employees engage with your customers and the way those customers share that experience.

ASSIGNMENT #11

Take out your menu and write a story about every single dish you sell. Tell me something interesting about it, and then identify which of these five areas it covers. Does the story justify price or give the diner some deeper appreciation for the restaurant or the ingredient? At the end you may find that there are a handful of items with no stories or perhaps weak stories. Think deeply about those items and decide how you can tell a more compelling story about them. If no story can be found, consider scrapping them altogether and replacing them with better dishes with more interesting stories.

Think back to the ABCD exercise. What are the stories only you can tell? Revisit those and figure out how they serve your business. Can you magnify those stories or find new ways to share them? How can you uncover (or manufacture) new stories that can help you better illustrate your value to the people you wish to serve?

CHAPTER 12

THE TRIANGLE PRINCIPLE

In some ways, marketing restaurants is the same as marketing any other product or service in the world. And yet there are key differences. I've tried to hammer home that point both on my podcast and throughout this book. For example, transactions last a long time in our business. We also sell more than the food we serve and collect much more than the money we charge. I've taught this hundreds of times to rooms full of restaurant owners, and to help illustrate my point, I've developed another framework. I call it the Triangle Principle.

MINDSET SHIFT
A successful marketing strategy must take into account three distinct areas: Attraction, Retention, and Evangelism.

The Triangle Principle states that each area—Attraction, Retention, Evangelism—requires a separate set of actions. Meaning, there should be *specific things you do* to achieve a *specific set of results*. Think about it. You need a reliable way to acquire new customers, right? That's Attraction. You need a consistent way to turn those first-time diners into repeat customers. That's Retention. And finally, you need to inspire each of those diners to spread the good word about your restaurant. I call that Evangelism. These are the three sides to my marketing triangle, and a cohesive strategy must include all of them.

The interesting thing is that most operators I meet begin with the first and rarely get to the others. "More butts in seats," they always tell me. And I understand where they're coming from. But don't forget the old adage: "It's cheaper to keep a customer than to go find a new one." If all you need are butts in seats, why should you care if those butts belong to people who have dined with you in the past? It seems obvious when you look at it that way, right? In fact, I'm going to let you in on a little secret: the Triangle Principle works best when done in reverse.

If you focus only on attracting new customers, you'll miss key opportunities to wow the guests you've already got. Instead, I want you to start with Evangelism. To be honest, we've spent a great deal of time on this already! Remember that most of your marketing will happen behind your back, so empower your servers and bartenders to be ambassadors for your brand and help them turn your diners into evangelists. Craft the experience in such a way that people can't help but snap photos and share the details of their experience; make it so they can't help but rave to their coworkers the next day at the office; make it so they just have to return with their parents the next time they're in town visiting. Make this specific and actionable. Like

I wrote earlier, there are specific things you can do to make these specific things happen. Often—and this may not sound sexy—these things are crafted. Manufactured.

Good food and good service is not a strategy; it's simply a prerequisite for going into business. You need something extra. Think of the Black Tap milkshakes. Over the past decade, they've become famous. Cookies and whipped cream and slices of cake towering high above the milkshake cup. They look so crazy that diners *just have to* take a picture and share it on social media. What happens then? Hundreds (or sometimes thousands) of other people see that photo, and it gets lodged in their brain. Maybe you've seen the pictures? Suddenly you remember it a few weeks from now when you're deciding where to go for dinner. Those milkshakes are incredible, you think, why not go check the place out? Of course, you have to order one just to see for yourself. And guess what? You then feel obligated to snap a picture and post it to your own feed. And over the next hour, hundreds (or sometimes thousands) of *your* followers will see your picture. And the cycle begins anew. This is how things go viral, when the guests begin evangelizing for the brand, reaching further than the brand possibly could on its own.

The very best restaurants will go out of their way to create these moments—manufacture them—to elicit some sort of reaction from their patrons. You need to do the same. There is no one way to do this, just as long as it gets done. Remember earlier when I explained that ABCD leads to E, and E stands for *everything*. Every choice you make communicates something to your target audience. You simply need to make sure that your communications are aligned and that you're creating moments that will wow the guest. My colleagues in the hotel industry call this *surprise and delight*; no wonder that, as an industry, they're better at this than we are.

If you want some more examples of this, check out David Burke's "Clothesline Bacon" or Alfred Portale's vertical presentation of Maine lobster from his days at Gotham Bar & Grill. Track down pictures of some of the "Pillow Dishes" at Alinea in Chicago or the five pound burger at Red Knapps in Rochester, Michigan. The internet is an incredible resource; you'll find no shortage of dishes that will make you stop and say, "Wow!" This is what we're going for when we're trying to spark word of mouth.

The second side of the triangle is Retention, and just like with Evangelism, there are specific actions you can take to convince someone to dine with you again. Sometimes it's as simple as asking them to come back or enticing them to return with a specific offer. Bounce-back promotions and business cards are two analog ways to accomplish this. Loyalty programs and email signups are good digital examples. And best of all, the dining experience itself has a lot to do with whether a guest will return sometime in the future. So do what you do best and make sure that the food, service, and decor inspire repeat visits. But don't assume that will be enough to get them to return. Make sure it's obvious to your guests that they are welcome—that you want them to come back—and give them reasons to find their way back to you.

We'll touch on this later on in the book, but I believe that an engaged email list is the most important asset a restaurant has at its disposal. You need to find a reliable way to capture your guests' information so that you can keep in touch with them down the line. Believe it or not, emails are a fairly reliable (and low cost) way of getting people to return. You simply need to put a system into place. The same is true with loyalty programs, social media marketing, branded apps, and bounce-back offers. They all work, but only if there's a strategy involved. Whatever you choose to do, make sure your actions are deliberate and measurable. You've done the hard work of getting them in the front door; it would be a crime to have them walk out and never return.

Finally, then, we come to Attraction, which (as I mentioned a moment ago) is really best saved for last. Why? Because it is the most complicated, the most time-consuming, and often the most expensive of the three. Raising awareness for your brand is getting harder each day. Hoping people will like your post and follow your social media account is more expensive than ever. And convincing people to move from the digital space to your real-world space can take a very, very long time. In advertising, the old guard had something they called the Rule of 7, which states that on average it takes seven impressions to even make an impression.[10] In reality, though, many now believe that number to be much higher given our increased exposure to advertising through newer digital channels.

Attraction may sound straightforward, though it's anything but. That's specifically why I saved it for last. And, in fact, it's important enough that I've dedicated all of Part Three to explaining it. External marketing is about finding ways to extend your reach beyond the four walls of your restaurant to make an impression on a would-be diner. In Part Three of this book, we'll talk about the best (and worst) ways to raise awareness for your brand. We'll talk about the customer journey, showing ways to ease your target audience down the sales funnel from awareness to interest to desire to action. Remember what we spoke about in the early chapters of this book: our people don't come to us to get fed. Food is sustenance, but if that's all they needed, they could do it cheaper and faster by cooking up some rice and beans at home. Desire is actually a good way of thinking about what we do. How do we make people want what we have? In the end, that's really the most important question we can answer. In the pages that follow, I'll show you some of the best ways I know to do that.

ASSIGNMENT #12

I want you to take out three pieces of paper. At the top of the first, write "Attraction." On the second, write "Retention." And on the third, write "Evangelism." I want you to think about what you're already doing to acquire new guests. Specifically, what are you doing to raise awareness for your brand and inspire people to come try you out. Those should all get listed on the Attraction page. On the Retention page, I want you to write down all the things you're doing to specifically get people to come back and dine with you again. Finally, on the third page, tell me all the things that inspire people to talk about their experience. Maybe it's a signature dish or a design flourish. Write down everything you can. And then, of course, I want you to add to the list. What are all the things you could—or should—be doing? This is how you begin to put a strategy in place.

PART THREE
EXTERNAL
MARKETING

CHAPTER 13

AWARENESS AND TRUST

So many restaurant owners I know seem to hold the same misguided belief that awareness is the key to success. "If people just knew we were here, then they'd line up out front." But isn't that just a version of the *Field of Dreams* effect I described earlier? The fact is, just because someone knows you exist, doesn't mean they're going to dine with you. Think of all the restaurants you pass by on your way to work. You know they're there, so why have you never gone inside half of them?

> **MINDSET SHIFT**
> The distance from obscurity to awareness
> is nowhere near as wide as the chasm
> between awareness and trust.

Simply getting on someone's radar is not enough. The hard work of marketing is to identify people who will be most apt to love what you do and then to convince them (over and over and over again) to trust you. And there's that T word again: trust. Hopefully by now you're seeing how important it is. Sometimes you'll hear marketers say that "people buy from companies that they know, like, and trust." It's one of those truisms that's gone unchanged for centuries. The key, then, is to get people to know you . . . so that you can get them to like you . . . so that in time they'll trust you enough to transact with you.

I hope you're seeing by now that this book is laid out in a deliberate way. The early lessons provided the foundation needed to have some of these more tactical conversations. We couldn't talk about customer acquisition until we defined positioning, and we couldn't discuss awareness and trust until we had a better understanding of value and price. Your company exists to solve a specific problem for a specific person at a specific moment in time. You need to show them that you're aware of their dilemma and have in fact crafted a compelling solution to help them.

As I've said many times already throughout this book, this is true no matter what type of product or service you're selling. Are you the answer to someone's prayers? If so, they will line up to buy from you. They will support you because you've gone out of your way to support them.

The Triangle Principle suggests that there are three areas all owners and operators need to focus on if they wish to build a successful marketing strategy: Attraction, Retention, and Evangelism. And remember that we always work backward. We do that because Attraction is the most difficult (and most expensive) of the three. Posting a nice picture on social media is not going to bring in droves of new diners; acquiring customers requires a more deliberate, comprehensive approach.

In marketing classes, they teach something called the AIDA Model. It's an acronym that stands for awareness, interest, desire, and action, describing the four levels a shopper passes through on their way to becoming a customer. It's also sometimes referred to as a sales funnel. Let's say we've taken our population—meaning all the people in a given market—and segmented that population to identify our target audience. (I showed you several ways to do this back in Chapter 2.) Right now, those people might be on our radar, but we are not yet on theirs. Our first job, then, is to make them aware of us. And there are many ways to do this.

A flashy sign might be enough to get attention . . . or a billboard on the side of the road. A direct mailer sent out to local residents might do the trick . . . or a sponsored ad targeting a group of individuals on Facebook. You could sponsor a local Little League team, host an open house, purchase a table at a local street fair, or participate in a charity dinner. All of those are ways to raise awareness for your brand. In reality, it's probably a combination of all of them and a hundred others I've not bothered to list here. The bottom line is this: Do what you can to stand out. Get reviewed. Get photographed. Cultivate friends in the neighborhood and make sure those people know that they're welcome in your restaurant. In the beginning, it's really just about making an impression on those you wish to serve.

But that alone is not enough. At least not for most people. Remember the Rule of 7? On average it takes about seven impressions for the brand to register with a potential customer. And that just measures brand recall. Meaning, will the diner remember the ad they saw a day later? A week later? A month later? In a world as saturated as this one, how can you find a way to set yourself apart from the competition? How can you stay top of mind with the people you seek to serve (your target audience) at the right moment (say, dinnertime)?

Once we've gotten their attention, we need to pique their interest. And again, there is no one way to do this. Depending on your concept, market, and audience, different tactics will be used. Right now you're simply trying to spark their curiosity, get them excited for what you're doing. In simple terms, you want them to take some further action besides chuckling at the funny jingle you created for your radio ad. This can be something as straightforward as visiting your website. So far, your sales funnel looks like this: the billboard (or flyer or radio ad) got their attention and prompted them to take further action (like visiting your website). Great!

We are working people down that sales funnel—from awareness to interest to desire to action. We'll get into this a bit later when we talk about digital presence, but it is now up to your website to close the deal. Everything should be aligned to get them to take some specific action, like reserving a table or placing an online order. Very rarely will someone see a Facebook post and click right away to purchase the product. Think about your own shopping habits. You might click on the ad, but your next step is probably to research the product line, check out the company's website, or seek out online reviews.

MINDSET SHIFT

Try to make it as easy as possible for someone to become a customer.

You need to put systems in place that help ease people down the funnel—effortlessly!—to a point where they can take action. Remember the old adage: people buy from companies that they know, like, and trust. You need to have a plan for each and every stage of the journey. And no, posting on social media once a day is not a strategy. It may be part of the strategy, but social media alone is not enough. You need an integrated, multipronged approach that acknowledges the diversity of your audience. "Meet them where they are," as the cliché goes.

Understanding how people come to you is important in understanding their unique customer journey. How do people first discover your restaurant? Word of mouth, advertisements, social media, reviews, best-of lists, etc.? Often a diner will need more information to make their decision, so you need to understand how they go about researching you. Let's say someone hears about your restaurant from one of their coworkers. What does that person do next? Maybe the conversation prompts them to check out your Instagram feed or to Google the restaurant. Or maybe they head to Yelp to read some reviews of the restaurant. What happens after that? If the Yelp reviews are good, maybe they click through to the website to check out your menu. As you can see, there are multiple paths that a diner can take to get to you. We simply need to understand what some of them may be and make it easy for them to become a paying customer.

Some companies—especially larger Fortune 500 firms—will create customer journey maps, laying out the five or ten most common paths that a shopper takes to become a customer. What's good about that is that you're forced to answer these four crucial questions:

- What does this person know about us at this point?
- What else do they need to know to be convinced?

- How can we make it obvious that this is the exact thing they've been seeking?
- How do we make it easy for them to transact?

A shopper requires specific things at each point in the sales funnel to move on to the next. Acknowledging that is the first step to helping your audience move from *curious and hungry* to *convinced and excited*. Building a pipeline of new customers is crucial to the long-term health of any business, but as you can see, it's a complicated proposition. That doesn't mean it's not worth the effort; you just need to be aware of the complexities and come to the table prepared.

ASSIGNMENT #13

I want you to take out a piece of paper and write "Awareness" across the top. Below, I want you to write down all the ways people have discovered your restaurant over the past twelve months. Bullet point the list and don't try to overthink things. If people see your sign as they drive by, simply write it down. If you think they saw your ad on the subway, write it down. Word of mouth? Add it to your paper. And so on. . . . Create an exhaustive list of all the possible ways you might've gotten on people's radar.

Next I want you to rate each one with a + or a –. Which ones do you think were best at getting people's attention? Why? Flip the page over, write down which ones worked for you, and try to explain why the others didn't quite work. Finally, I want you to write down five to ten new ideas for how you might be able to get some attention. What would have to happen to put those into practice?

Take out a second page and write "Interest" across the top. Where do people go to learn more about you? To see your menu, scope out your dining room, or find out what other people think of the place? Bullet point those things and again write a + or – next to each one. Flip the page over and tell me which ones did the best job at enticing prospective diners to take action. Why are the others falling short? Finally, as before, come up with ways you can improve this stage of the sales funnel. What else can you do to ease people into taking action?

Finally, then, on a third piece of paper write "Action" across the top. What is the specific action you want people to take when they engage with your brand? Book a reservation? Order online? Something else? What are the specific ways you can make that frictionless? How can you make it easier for people to become customers? Write down your answers.

CHAPTER 14
PROMISE

D ay in and day out, businesses make promises with their customers. The merchant *promises* to deliver a result, and the
consumer then chooses whether they want to believe that *promise*.
Your job as an operator is to understand the result the consumer is
seeking, craft a product that can deliver on that promise, and then
articulate that clearly to the consumer. This is why it's so hard to
be all things to all people. Choices are such that they require us to
pick this or that, quiet or loud, expensive or cheap, salty or sweet.
You can't open a sports bar and expect couples to come in to celebrate their anniversaries. Likewise you can't expect a commuter
running late for work to wait longer than a couple of minutes for
a bagel sandwich on their way to the train.

MINDSET SHIFT
At the heart of every transaction is a promise.

If you have a candlelit dining room with soft music and fine china, you're making a specific promise with a specific customer looking for a specific kind of experience. Couples looking for that kind of experience will be elated when they arrive to enjoy a romantic dinner. All your marketing exists to help communicate specific things to specific people. The promise needs to be clearly stated, and the experience needs to make good on that promise. Each and every decision you make builds trust with a potential diner. Remember that ABCD leads to E, and E stands for *Everything*. Every choice you make communicates something to the consumer. It is the thread woven through everything we do as marketers.

This process takes a long time. You can't just show someone a commercial and expect them to believe you. People are more wary than that, especially when it comes to their hard-earned money. As I pointed out earlier, people buy from companies that they know, like, and trust. One Facebook ad isn't going to convince them to trust you. In the beginning it's just about introducing yourself—making them aware of who you are and what you do. In time, as they get to know you, they may start to like you. That's good. You're easing them down the sales funnel. The last piece is trust—as we've spoken about in previous chapters—and this has everything to do with the promise you make to the consumer. Your website communicates something. So do your social media feeds. The food you serve, the way you plate that food, and the prices you charge for that food all communicate something to a prospective diner. You are telling them what sort of experience you provide—promising to deliver a certain result—and then asking them to trust that you'll come through.

A diner might check out your website and *want* to believe you, but many will need more information to be convinced. This is why we market. It's difficult to know how a customer will come to us or to know what they'll need to believe what we're telling them. Do they discover new restaurants on social media, or do they prefer to run a simple Google search? Do they trust Yelp reviews or the local food critic? Or is it all word of mouth for them? Perhaps they rely on a small group of confidants when choosing their next great meal. We can't just put up a great website and trust people will find it. We can't just post beautiful pictures to Instagram and trust that they'll be enough to convince people to book a reservation. We need an integrated marketing strategy that can articulate that promise no matter how a potential diner hears about us, and every piece of communication needs to hammer home that promise.

A great website allows you to *tell your story in the way you wish it told.* It's a powerful tool, but most consumers don't believe everything a company tells them. You certainly don't. And neither do I. My curiosity might be piqued by a restaurant's website, but before I reserve a table (or make a purchase or book a trip), I'm probably going to do a bit more legwork. I might check out some online reviews or ask around with some of my colleagues. I might Google the restaurant to see some pictures of the dining room or wander into a Facebook Group to ask around. Your customers do the same thing. So you need to be everywhere, and you need to be consistent in your messaging.

Consistency will be a big part of your success. The reason my son jumps off the dock and into my arms is because he trusts me. After two hundred jumps into the lake, he knows I have never let him go. And so he's eager to jump again and again. One of the best ways to get someone to believe you is to show them all the times you've already kept your word. This is what word of mouth is all about. There are people who have already experienced your restaurant, people who can attest to the fact that the business does in fact deliver on the promise.

That is why word of mouth is so powerful. It's why every guest matters, every table matters. If a guest has a bad meal, others are sure to find out about it. Even if that guest doesn't go around broadcasting it, someone will eventually ask their opinion. And inevitably that guest will share their opinion.

Your music is part of the promise. So is your service style. The signage out front communicates something to the folks driving by, promising a certain kind of experience. The question is whether the complete experience is making good on that promise. At the end of the day what we're really talking about here are the guests' expectations, and that's a good place for us to be. Why? Because it means we're thinking about the people we're serving.

My very first boss here in New York told me something that changed the way I thought about restaurants. It led to a profound shift in the way I go about my work, and it's influenced the way I talk about marketing to this day . . .

MINDSET SHIFT
Hospitality is all about exceeding
the guests' expectations.

But to exceed someone's expectations, you need to understand what they're expecting in the first place. Your marketing efforts are about setting those expectations—making sure you're communicating the right message to the right people, the kind of people who will love what you do. *For those who are STRUGGLING with a problem, we promise our product will SOLVE that problem.* But then your goal as an operator should be to meet those expectations (the promise!) and to exceed those expectations. That way, even if you fall short, you will have still kept your word.

ASSIGNMENT #14

What is the promise you make with your guests? Write it down. This goes hand in hand with the work you did earlier in this book. Get crystal clear on the problem you're solving for your audience, and make sure you understand what makes you uniquely qualified to solve it. Go through your business and make sure everything is aligned to tell the same story—to make good on that promise. Where are the holes? Identify some ways for you to plug those holes.

CHAPTER 15

PRESENCE

n 1942 Joseph Schumpeter coined the term *creative destruction*, referring to the effect that innovation has on a free market. The theory basically says that new technologies (and products and services and ideas) will always continue to replace outdated ones.[11] Progress only moves in one direction, and the mere act of creation is in itself destructive. This realization is as profound today as it was back then. In fact, we're living through something of a capitalistic golden age. What am I talking about?

The internet, of course. It has fundamentally reshaped our world over the past three decades, replacing almost every single tool we once used as marketers. Think about how much has changed in your life over the past thirty years, and consider how much of that is due to the rise of the internet. The Yellow Pages has been replaced by Google, travel agents have given way to Expedia, television is being eaten alive by the streaming services, and shopping malls lay empty as e-commerce becomes more cost-effective and efficient than ever before. Travel, education, medicine, retail, fitness, news, sports, and more—all have been fundamentally reshaped by the internet.

We're more than halfway through the book, and it would be impossible to go any further without acknowledging the effect that digital technology has had on our industry. The way owners promote their restaurants has changed largely because the way our guests search for restaurants has changed. And in a place as vast as the internet, you need a reliable way to be found.

At this point you should know who you are and who you're for. You have identified your key competitors and now understand how you differ from each of them. You've taken stock of your marketing efforts—both internal and external—and grasp the importance of communicating your value to the audience you seek to serve. If you've been following along with the assignments at the end of each chapter, you've already done all of this. You're in a great position now to tackle this next part.

The new challenge is to communicate your value with tools that might not come as naturally to you on platforms that aren't quite as effective as the dinner plate. Your menu should be able to communicate your value to a diner—same with the service they get and the room they're sitting in. But what about the folks sitting at home on their couch scrolling on their phones? How do they know the burger is juicy and delicious if they can't taste it? How do they know your dining room is romantic if they've never been there to experience it? This may sound obvious, but so much of your job is about translating the dining experience to those who have not yet experienced it. This gets to the heart of fortifying your digital presence.

Lucky for us, we live in extraordinary times, and it's never been cheaper or easier to do. What follows is by no means an exhaustive list (I could fill four books just covering this topic); instead, I want you to think of this as a jumping-off point—a way to get you thinking about how your brand exists in the digital world.

WEBSITE

It all begins and ends with your website. I say that because the website is often the diner's first or last impression of your brand. So make it count! Think of the website as your digital home—an extension of your restaurant. How do you want people to feel when they walk in the front door? You've got to figure out a way to elicit the same emotion when they land on your homepage. Where do you want them to go once they arrive? It should be obvious on the website as well as in the restaurant.

Web design is like fashion; it's always changing. So I won't waste my time talking about what's popular right now; I will undoubtedly be wrong by the time this book goes to print. I will, however, talk to you about some fundamentals of good web design. Here are five truisms that will probably never change:

1. Your website exists for one reason and one reason only: to convince the user to take action. You must understand what it is you want people to do and then make sure everything is properly aligned to get people to take that specific action.
2. Think carefully about who is visiting this site and where they came from. By that I mean, what do they already know about you, and what else do they need to know to take action?
3. Clarity is a lost art. Make sure every sentence, every image, every page helps clarify the message you wish to

communicate so that the user can easily make the decision you want them to make and—as stated above—take the action you wish them to take.

4. Less is more. Don't feel compelled to share your whole life story. Give people just enough to get them excited, just enough to become customers. You'll have more time to educate them when they're sitting in your dining room.

5. Finally, make the experience as frictionless as possible. At every point, figure out if there's a simpler solution, a more streamlined path to get the user to where you need them to go.

SEARCH ENGINES

This will probably come as no surprise to you, but according to Semrush, Google was the number one website in the world in January 2023 with more than one hunded billion monthly hits. YouTube (which is owned by Google) came in second with a little over eighty-six billion monthly hits, and Facebook was a distant third with about thirteen billion hits.[12]

Simply put, the internet is where people go to find things. Your job, then, as a business owner, is to make sure you're found by the people who are looking for the kind of experience you provide. Google's entire business, in fact, is built on connecting merchants and consumers—people with problems and those who have crafted solutions to those problems. Relevancy is the name of the game, and you simply need to make sure your business pops up when it matters most. In the example above, you need to make sure the web knows what you do so they know when to suggest your business.

Luckily your website has a lot to do with whether you're found or not. (It's why we covered it first!) You know who you are and who you're for, so make sure that's obvious in the copy you use and the images you choose to share.

Search engine optimization (SEO) is a science at this point, and we don't really have the time to dig into it here. So I'll simply say this: if you're more interested in going deep into the subject, there are great resources out there. Simply type your question into the Google search bar, and you'll find a ton of online tools to help you. However, the five steps below will give you the foundation you need to get started:

1. You can do yourself a big favor and claim your Google My Business page (google.com/business). This, more than just about anything else, will determine your success when it comes to organic search. Fill out all the information and be sure to keep that information current. Post from time to time and make sure to respond to each and every user review. (More on that later in this chapter.)

2. Track your NAP credentials across the entire internet. NAP is an acronym that stands for "name," "address," and "phone" . . . and, actually, postpandemic I like to include "hours" as well. So I guess we can use our own acronym—NAPH. You'd be surprised how many business owners skip this step, but you need to make sure this information matches across the entire internet.

3. Optimize your headers, title tags, URL slugs, metadata, and page content. Simply put, make sure the page headers match the page content and that the URL and metadata are consistent. If you're designing the menu page of your

website, make sure you put "Menu" at the top of the page and use an obvious web address like myrestaurant.com/menu. Metadata is a technical part of web design, where brief descriptions live on the back end of each page with the sole purpose of helping sites like Google understand what that page is all about. If you're working with a developer, simply ask them to show you what they're doing with metadata tags so you can confirm it's being done.

4.   Keep your website "alive." Google likes to see that things change from time to time. On the podcast, I've often suggested that operators house a blog on their website. This gives you a perfect opportunity to talk about the things you're doing in the restaurant, but it also keeps the site "alive." As it turns out, this is beneficial when it comes to ranking higher in search results.

5.   Make sure your website is mobile-friendly. More and more you'll hear the experts recommend a mobile-first strategy, which simply means that you should design for the mobile experience before you even consider how the site performs on a desktop computer. This, I've found, is generally good advice.

SOCIAL MEDIA

Love it or hate it, social media is here to stay, but most people don't have the right perspective when it comes to these platforms. Let me explain. Just like with websites, social media is changing all the time—not only which platforms are most popular but the ways in which each platform operates. Rather than share best practices (run a simple Google search for those), I'm going to focus instead on five common threads worth acknowledging:

1. You don't own these platforms, so in the end you don't own your followers or the relationships you build with them on those platforms. Meaning, if the sites suddenly shut down one day, you no longer have a way to connect with those 2,000 followers or 10,000 followers or 100,000 followers. This is also true every time the algorithm changes. Use the sites to your advantage, but be vigilant about driving people *from* social media *over to* the platforms you do own (like your website or email list).

2. Stay nimble. These platforms are always rolling out new tools and features. Follow the trends, watch what's working across the various platforms, and don't let yourself get stuck in a rut. The things that worked last year probably aren't working this year. Acknowledge, accept, and adapt.

3. Make sure the visual identity and brand voice are aligned with your brand promise. The website should be an extension of the actual dining experience, and your social media presence should be an extension of the identity you've built on your website.

4. It's called social media for a reason. *Be social.* These platforms give you unfettered access to both existing and prospective customers. Find opportunities to engage with them in ways that feel authentic to you and your brand. If you treat it as a digital billboard, you're missing many of the key benefits these platforms provide.

5. You need to implement both an organic and a paid social strategy. If you're not taking advantage of the advertising

opportunities on these platforms, you're missing one of their key benefits. Aside from everything else they do, these sites are the most sophisticated advertising platforms ever created. They allow you to segment and target people better than ever before. Make sure you're using those tools to promote your brand.

REVIEW SITES

I once did a podcast episode titled "Y-E-L-P is a four-letter word." For years this site was the bane of my existence (yours too, I'm sure), but I've come to embrace the democratization of restaurant criticism. No longer does a single critic wield all the power. Instead, people are turning to alternative channels for advice on where to eat. At the end of the day, I think that's good for everyone. Sites like Yelp, Tripadvisor, Foursquare, and Google are places where diners can go to leave reviews about their experiences. It's also, then, a place where prospective diners can go to research restaurants before they commit to making a reservation.

This area of marketing is referred to as *reputation management*. There are companies that will aggregate your reviews for you and even respond on your behalf. And if you don't have the time to manage this yourself, by all means go and explore some of those options. But it's still worth knowing some best practices. Again, here are five tips worth considering:

1. You've already claimed your Google My Business page. You now need to do the same on Yelp, Tripadvisor, and

Foursquare. Fill out all the information so that it matches and it's correct.

2. Monitor these sites on a weekly basis and put a system in place for tracking all the reviews you get. Figure out who is compiling them each week and whose job it is to respond.

3. That leads us nicely into this: as a business, you must respond to each and every review. Keep your responses brief! For the positive reviews, simply thank them for the kind words and tell them you can't wait to have them back. As for the bad reviews, don't debate or try to justify whatever happened. Simply acknowledge the situation, apologize, and thank them for taking the time to share feedback. I'll often close with something like this, "We appreciate the time you took to share your feedback. This is how we improve! Please contact me at (insert email address) if you have any further details you'd like to share about your experience." You do this not necessarily to win these people back but to show everyone else who's looking at these reviews that you're a conscientious owner who cares.

4. Encourage diners to leave positive reviews. If there are people in the restaurant having a great time, make sure to remind them to log a review on one of these sites. Simply explain that this is one of the most powerful tools available to an independent restaurant and that their opinions really do matter.

5. Pull some quotes from the very best reviews and use them as testimonials on your website, social media platforms, in the bottom of an email, or wherever you think makes sense. As is so often the case, perception really is reality.

If you're getting some love, make sure to share it with the people who might care to know.

Digital strategy could be its own book—and there are certainly plenty out there if you're interested. My goal was not to give you a step-by-step game plan but instead to shift the way you may be thinking about your online presence. For any brick-and-mortar restaurant, the steps I outlined above are a must. Do those, and you'll be miles ahead of the competition. And when you're ready for more, check out my reading list at the end of the book. You'll find a couple of good deep dives on the subject, and if that still isn't enough to satisfy your needs, you can always check out the *Restaurant Strategy* podcast. This is a topic we cover often.

ASSIGNMENT #15

Go through each of the four areas we covered in this chapter and address each of the five bullet points. Set simple goals for yourself and then put a plan in place to track your efforts. Monitor the results to see how things begin to change after three, six, and nine months.

CHAPTER 16

PERMISSION

I n textbooks you'll often read about the Four Ps of Marketing. They are product, price, promotion, and place. Together they are referred to as the *marketing mix*, a framework first developed in the 1950s as a way of thinking about how to bring a product to market.[13] But for my money, I find the whole thing a bit stiff and outdated. That's why I put together my own framework, the ABCDs of Marketing, and followed that up with the Triangle Principle. Both of those—in my humble opinion—better articulate how you need to think about the product you've created and how you're going to share that with the audience you seek to serve.

But that's not to say I don't love alliteration. Because I do. And these three chapters (this one and the two previous) outline something I like to call the Three Ps of Trust Building: promise, presence, and permission. As we discussed earlier in the book, people buy from companies that they know, like, and trust. And the gap between awareness and desire is nowhere near as wide as the chasm between desire and trust. The picture you post online may inspire a "like," but will it get the user to open their favorite delivery app and place an order? If the answer is no, do you know why? Is your promise clearly defined? Does the consumer believe that you're going to keep that promise? Does your online presence help to articulate the promise you're making with your audience? Those questions get to the heart of the trust we are trying to build with our audiences. Ultimately, what we're looking for is the last P—permission.

Until about thirty years ago, there was only one kind of marketing. These days it's often referred to as *interruption marketing*. This is where the consumer is looking at something that *she wants to see*, and the marketer interrupts that activity to show her something that *they want her to see*. She's reading a magazine article, then flips the page only to be interrupted by a perfume ad. She's driving her car upstate and the beauty of nature is broken up by cheesy billboards dotting the horizon. She's watching TV and every eight minutes has to sit through a barrage of insurance commercials.

For hundreds of years, this was the only real way for marketers to reach an audience. Then something incredible happened. Email was invented and with it came a whole new way of operating. We were suddenly more connected than ever before, both to the people we loved and to the companies we supported. Before long, those companies discovered the power of permission. Seth Godin first coined the term with the release of his 1999 bestseller, *Permission Marketing*, and later defined it in one of his most popular blog posts: "Permission marketing is the privilege (not the right) of delivering anticipated, personal, and relevant messages to people who actually want to get them."[14]

MINDSET SHIFT
Permission helps you shift
from "push" to "pull."

Remember that the first part of the Triangle Principle is Attraction. That's not an accident. I believe our job as marketers is to draw people in—to make sure they know where to find the solution to their problem. And this is not a new thing. The late-night infomercials of the eighties and nineties were probably the first example of permission marketing. Instead of short advertisements wedged in between regular programming, the infomercial *was* the entertainment. They weren't interrupting anything; they were the main event. Superstars like Ron Popeil adapted their showroom sales techniques for television audiences: "But wait, there's more!" Just as you were about to change the channel, the host would *pull you back in*. They would show you everything you'd get, making obvious the value their product provided—before going one step further. It's not all that different from what we do in restaurants, right?

Here's the power of permission marketing: Someone has told you that not only do they like you and your product but also they would like to hear more about your products in the future. They've given you permission to market to them! This puts you in a powerful position. Once you have permission, you can skip past all the convincing and get right to the offer. You have already done the hard work of building trust; now you simply have to show them the new solutions you've created.

The people on your list know you, like you, and trust you enough to give over their personal information. They've either purchased from you in the past or are seriously considering purchasing from you in the future. And you now have an efficient, relatively inexpensive way of communicating with them. This is an incredible shift, and it's all thanks to technology. Since much of the hard work has already been done, now you simply have to nurture that relationship. Makes sense, right? Of course! So then, how do you do it?

Remember, you want people on your list so that you can sell to them. Which begs the question: Why would *they* want to be on your list? As is the case with much of the material we've covered so far, there is no one way to do it. But the key is to give so much value to your audience that they look forward to hearing from you. And then—once you've built up equity—you can ask them for something. By that point you will have given so much away, that they will be more than open to your offer.

I've said this many times before on the podcast, but it bears repeating here: an engaged email list is a restaurant's most valuable asset. If you don't have one yet, you need to take the following three steps:

CHOOSE AN EMAIL SERVICE PROVIDER.

There are literally hundreds of companies out there to choose from, but Mailchimp is the company I always love to recommend. The stylish templates and drag-and-drop interface make it very easy to use, plus there are all kinds of great tools for segmenting the list and retargeting based on behavior, identity, geography, and more. It is the easiest and most cost-effective option out there, but by all means . . . you choose. As I said, there are tons of companies that offer a similar service, like Constant Contact, Emma, Klaviyo, etc. Just make sure you start the account today!

START GROWING THAT LIST.

You need a reliable way to grow your email list, so come up with a plan, put someone in charge of it, then hold them accountable. I did an entire episode about this on the podcast (episode #51), but to get started, here are the three easiest ways to start collecting email addresses: First, every Monday import the contacts from your POS and reservation software. Second, put a pop-up on your website and an email capture in the footer. Finally, when you drop the check, invite your guests to sign up for your list. By all means you can incentivize this, just as long as you capture their info. You can go old school with a comment card or do it digitally with a tablet, QR code, NFC tag, or loyalty program opt-in. All that matters is that you do it.

SEND WEEKLY COMMUNICATIONS.

Challenge yourself in the beginning to send one email a week. Make a spreadsheet (otherwise known as a marketing calendar) to figure out what you're going to talk about each week. Remember the 1:1:1 Principle: one email, one subject, one call to action. This week you'll talk about the new salmon dish you just added to the menu; next week remind people about booking private events; the following week you can talk about some charity dinner you're hosting; and after that you can talk about your signature margarita. Whatever it is, just make sure you're providing value to the people you're engaging with. *Why would they want to be on our list?* Every email you send should help to answer that question.

Do these three things, and you'll begin changing the connection you have with your guests. It becomes less transactional and more relationship driven. And that's exactly what you want. Again, it's all about building trust! You don't marry someone without getting to know them first, and you don't spend your hard-earned cash at a place you don't trust. If the primary action you're looking to drive is an order (or reservation), then the secondary action should be an email signup. Yes, it really is that important. And once people give you permission to contact them, by all means . . . do it!

ASSIGNMENT #16

Follow the three steps outlined and get started with email marketing. If you're already sending out regular emails, then use this as an opportunity to audit your current efforts. Is your list growing in a consistent way? Are you packing your emails with value? Get to a place where the answer is YES to both of those questions so that your audience continues to give you permission to market to them. Then nurture that relationship and let it breed deeper loyalty for your brand.

CHAPTER 17

CONTENT IS KING

The average American adult sees thousands—literally thousands—of advertisements every single day. TV commercials, billboards, banner ads, radio spots, social media posts, plus logos on passing shirts, hats, bags, and more. It's exhausting! Yet as marketers we must find a way to cut through the noise.

And by the way, let's first agree that not taking action is not an option. If you're going to sell a product or service, you need to let people know about it. The key is to do it in a way that grabs attention, builds trust, and inspires action. There are a million bad ways to do this (surely you can think of a few right off the top of your head). It's far more difficult these days to find good examples because when it's done well, it's much harder to see.

Successful marketing feels natural, almost obvious. The case is made in such an effortless way that it hardly feels like selling at all. Think about the iPhone. Apple doesn't get into a shouting match with the rest of the market; they pull consumers in with a whisper. That's because the product they're marketing really is that good.

But there is a parallel in our business.

> **MINDSET SHIFT**
> If you have to shout, it might mean your
> product isn't worth talking about.

This goes hand in hand with the advice I shared in the opening sentences of this book. We don't need *just another* anything. Not another sports bar. Not another sushi counter. We've all had enough sweet-and-sour pork to last a lifetime, and please, oh, please, not another steakhouse. We've got enough of everything, except the thing we've never had before. I challenge you to do something original.

Bring yourself fully to the business and make your restaurant a reflection of who you are and what you believe. Originality is the most important ingredient for success—either in concept, execution, or the way you position yourself in the market. You've hopefully internalized the early lessons from this book and are ready to share your brand with the world. Great!

Restaurants these days need to think of themselves as mini media companies, putting out high-quality content on a consistent basis. Like it or not, it's just the way our world works. But that doesn't mean you can put out crap. Quality over quantity, always. And even though I said consistency matters, you get to define the cadence of your communications.

There are all kinds of different ways to connect with your audience, and one channel is never enough. What we want is to build a relationship with our customers (or prospective customers) so that they begin to anticipate those communications. Again, consider the difference between *interrupting* your customers and *earning permission.*

You're going to have to start taking a holistic approach to your communication strategy. You can't just snap a pretty picture of a steak, post it online, and expect it to drive hordes of hungry people into your restaurant. They call that the *spray and pray* approach to marketing: "If I can post enough pretty pictures on the internet and make enough people hungry, some of them are surely bound to come in."

And man, oh, man is that the wrong way to go about this. I don't know if you've noticed, but there are a lot of juicy steaks on the internet these days. Even if you did succeed, you'd be wasting a lot of energy and money. Better to build a real strategy—one that's measurable and repeatable.

When you set up a post (or a billboard or an email), you need to understand what that given communication is trying to achieve. Again, start thinking of yourself as a mini media company. Let's use CNN as an example. Throughout the day they have regular news programs where the goal is to "inform" their viewers. In the evening they have programming to "incite debate" featuring political pundits who share their opinions on the day's headlines. And then they also have fully produced shows that exist to "entertain" the audience. They all serve different purposes at different times of day for different segments of their audience. They vary their programming to engage viewers all day long.

You must do the same sort of thing in your restaurant. Mind you, I'm not talking about twenty-four-hour programming. But you should be utilizing all your different channels to connect with your guests. Start by identifying each of the channels at your disposal:

- Website
- Email
- Text messaging
- Social media
- Direct mail
- Mass media advertising

We'll start by addressing the elephant in the room. Mass media—meaning television, radio, large-scale print campaigns, etc.—is out of reach for most independent restaurant owners. You'll bankrupt yourself just trying to compete with the larger budgets that many of the big chains have. And you know what? Fine. Let them have it. I prefer the other channels anyway. Why? Because all the others allow us to track the results.

That's the thing about TV. It's almost impossible to measure a commercial's success. But I can measure impressions and engagement on a Facebook ad and track open rates on emails and click-throughs on texts. I can tweak my website to optimize session time and bounce rate and rework the copy on my landing page to improve conversions. How can you tell if a commercial works? Ad agencies are still using antiquated measurements like *brand lift* and *ad recall* to put their clients at ease.

As we wade into the waters of content creation, I want you to think about three things: identity, voice, and differentiation. We'll come back to those at the end of the chapter, but again, just like we spoke about earlier in the book, you will succeed by understanding your audience and figuring out how you fit into your market. Or, more appropriately, how you can *stand out* in your market. Every piece of communication must acknowledge and articulate who you are and what sort of value you provide. If you understand that—as you should by now—it's simply a matter of hammering it home so that the consumer understands it.

The world of digital marketing moves way too fast for me to write about it in a book. By the time you put your hands on the book, anything I wrote would be at least three to six months out of date. That's why I've got the podcast! It's a far better medium for that sort of information. Instead of discussing specific tactics (which change all the time), I want to make sure you understand the strategies involved.

CAPTURE

Specific platforms may come and go and the way we use those platforms might change, but what I'm absolutely certain of is this: you will need to put a system into place to capture high-quality content on a consistent basis. It doesn't matter whether you shoot everything yourself or if you outsource it to an agency partner. You need a reliable way to collect content. Look at your calendar and commit to a photo shoot once a week or once a month even. But don't skip it. Same with videos. Find a way to capture content. Do it as often as you can, and don't worry about fancy equipment. As long as the lighting is good, your smartphone will serve you quite well.

ORGANIZATION

Next, you need a secure place to store all this content you're capturing and a system for organizing everything. There's fancy media storage software out there that will let you tag and search images and videos all kinds of different ways. Or for less than twenty dollars per month, you can just get a Dropbox subscription. Either one will work just fine, as long as you commit to using it—and commit to keeping it organized.

COLLABORATION

As the saying goes, two heads are better than one. Just like a great idea can come from anywhere, the same is true with content. Even the most gifted photographer isn't going to be able to capture every moment in a restaurant. My guess is that nearly every person you employ has a smartphone in their pocket; so empower your team to be part of the solution. If they see something worth capturing, they should be empowered to whip out their phone and film it.

Tell them what sort of material you're looking for and the best way to share it with the marketing team. And by the way, I know that the "marketing team" might just be you. Just make sure everyone knows how to upload a photo to the shared drive, tag it appropriately, and give some details in the caption. I promise you that people will be more excited—and more engaged in their work—if you let them bring a little creativity to the table.

With this full roster of amateur photographers and videographers (i.e., your staff) at your disposal, you're going to get a ton of material. Figure out who's good on camera and have them go live. Figure out who's got a knack for editing and have them splice new footage together. Figure out what sort of talent is hiding in plain sight and make sure they feel a part of the process. Best of all, you'll then be able to use the professionals you hire in a much more targeted way to create the kind of content your team can't.

DISTRIBUTION

Take a top-level view of your marketing efforts by separating out all the different channels. In the end they will be integrated—you'll fortify the messaging on your website with e-blasts and social media posts; the wording on your pop-up email capture will echo the copy on your postcards—but for now, I want you to compartmentalize things. Make sure you have a system in place for each of your channels. Who decides what goes on the website? Who does the actual updating? Who reviews that content and how frequently? Who writes the copy for the e-blasts? Who decides the frequency of those communications? Who takes photos for Instagram? Who edits the reels? Who is responsible for outlining the content calendar? Even if you decide to work with an agency, someone will have to oversee them. Figure out who that person is and what sort of system needs to be put into place.

Finally, think back to the Triangle Principle we discussed in Part Two of the book. Which channels are you utilizing to raise awareness for your brand? To get attention? How are you using that attention to identify potential customers? What actions are you specifically taking to get people to sign up, order online, or reserve a table? How are you turning that first visit into a return visit? What are you doing to ensure that repeat customers become regulars? How will these regulars know what to say about you to their friends and family? To their coworkers and old college buddies? How can you prompt them to do so?

If your product is differentiated, then it shouldn't be that hard to identify the key traits that set you apart from your competitors. Brand voice and identity are the way we make those differences obvious. Knowing your value is one thing; communicating that value is quite another. If you're opening a lively tapas restaurant, then you need to find unique ways to say that. Remember—ABCD leads to E, and E stands for *everything*. Every choice you make communicates something to a prospective diner. You put out content to help tell your own story. Those images and little snippets of video communicate your promise and help anchor your brand in the minds of the consumers. Everything you do matters. Everything you put out into the world helps to build trust and convince people of the value you provide.

You may grumble at the prospect of having to do this, but let me reframe this for you. At no point in the history of human civilization has it been easier to target the people you want to reach and tell your story. Your phone now doubles as a camera and a megaphone. Figure out what you want to say and then find all the different ways to say it

---

MINDSET SHIFT
Get attention. Build trust. Inspire action.

This is the second mantra I'm sharing with you. Pin it to your wall and repeat those six words anytime you feel stuck. As an owner, almost everything you do needs to accomplish one of those three things. You just need to be clear on which one you're doing at any given point in time. Because guess what? A single communication will almost never accomplish more than one at a time. How do you learn to say exactly what you mean? Keep reading.

ASSIGNMENT #17

Take out several pieces of blank paper. At the top of each one, write down one of your marketing channels. Email should be one. Website should be another. Instagram? Write it down. Facebook? Take out another sheet. One for each and every one of your channels. Anything you use to communicate to your audience gets a page. In-store collateral, internal communications, direct mailers, and so on. Below, I want you to explain the system that's currently in place for that channel. For your email marketing, I want to know who comes up with the cadence and content for your weekly communications. Who writes the copy? Who edits? Who is responsible for tracking the metrics? And how do you measure your success with that channel? Do that for each and every channel. By the end you might find that some channels have a clear system in place, while others have hardly anything at all. Perfect. (The first step is acknowledging you have a problem.) Your next job will be to bring them all up to par.

CHAPTER 18

WHAT I MEANT
TO SAY WAS . . .

According to *Time* magazine, the average attention span of an American adult is now less than that of a goldfish. Researchers at Microsoft surveyed 2,000 participants and studied the brain activity of 112 others using electroencephalograms (EEGs). They found that since the year 2000 (about when the mobile revolution began), the average attention span has dropped from twelve seconds to eight. And while that might not sound like much, it represents the single biggest drop ever recorded.[15] And so what does that mean for us as marketers? Simply that we must be more efficient with our communications to be effective.

Originally this was going to be a chapter all about copywriting, but I realized just a few sentences in that that would have been a complete oversight. Words are just one piece of how we communicate with others. Images, video, sound, color, texture, smell, and taste are all equally as important. Think of each one as a weapon in your arsenal—a tool you use to get the job done. In this case, your job is to share your message with those who most need to hear it. Sometimes a headline says it all. Other times, even the right words aren't enough.

Practicing what I preach, I've structured this chapter a bit differently from the others. What follows is a series of quick tips I've picked up during my time spent marketing restaurants:

WRITING

- Say what you mean and mean what you say. Learn to be specific and articulate.
- Less is more. Never use twelve words when eleven will do.
- Spelling counts, and grammar matters more than you think. Go purchase a copy of Strunk and White's classic *The Elements of Style* and keep it handy. Computers these days come preloaded with software to assist, but in the end, you should be able to tell the difference between good and bad writing.
- Every piece of content should serve a specific purpose. That's true of an email, a blog post, or the descriptions you use on your menu. Understand what you're trying to accomplish and do not waver in your pursuit of that singular goal.
- Understand your audience and make sure you are speaking only to them. Most of the writing you do will be intimate—an email, a social media caption, a menu—rather than great oratory. If you're delivering a speech, then yes, you need

to dig deep for some of that lofty prose. For the rest, you just need to tell your audience what they need to know.

- Be judicious with adjectives. Using too many descriptors when referring to yourself, your restaurant, or your food is akin to laughing at your own jokes.
- I touched briefly on this in Chapter 16, but don't forget the 1:1:1 Principle: one email, one message, one call to action. Tell people what they can expect by opening the email, make good on that promise, then tell them how to take action.
- If you're landing a joke (or making a point), the most surprising (or emphatic) word should come at the end. Your sentence should pull the reader forward until they reach the most important part of your message.
- Words have rhythm, a cadence. Just like a meal has a natural ebb and flow, so too does any piece of good writing. Find breath in your work and embrace the space between the words.
- Always use the active (rather than passive) voice. Passive voice: "A Harvest Dinner will be held on Sunday, October 3, at Restaurant XYZ." Active voice: "Restaurant XYZ is hosting a Harvest Dinner on Sunday, October 3." It's a small shift that makes a huge impact when it comes to readability.
- If the goal of any piece of content is to inspire action, first consider what the reader needs to know to take that desired action. Communicate that as simply and succinctly as possible to make the process as frictionless as possible.

PHOTOGRAPHY

- Always try to fill the frame with food. The viewer cares less about the table setting than they do the garnish.

- Food photography has just one objective: to make people hungry. The viewer needs to immediately recognize the subject matter so that they can quickly have the thought, "Wow, that looks delicious!" If the viewer struggles—even for a second—to identify what exactly they're looking at, they will never get to that all-important second statement.

- The human eye is drawn to patterns. They put us at ease and help us make sense of unfamiliar surroundings and objects. Find patterns in your composition every time you line up a shot. If none exist, create some.

- Undercook all proteins and vegetables that are going to be photographed. Don't sauce a dish until the moment you're ready to shoot. Save garnishes for the very last second. Keep a small bowl of oil and a brush nearby to give the food a little glisten between shots.

- Before you replate a dish that isn't working, try changing your relationship to the food. Get higher. Get lower. Spin the plate around. Change the table setup. Move the lighting. Add props to the setup. Then—if all else fails—experiment with the layout on the plate.

- When shooting a restaurant, you need either an empty dining room or a full one. Anything in between will not work. Try for yourself if you don't believe me.

- Dining room shots require a special attention to detail. If done right you'll spend an hour getting the room ready and ten minutes actually shooting.

VIDEO

- There's a reason they yell "Action!" on a movie set. Pouring, slicing, shaking, folding, mixing, searing, plating, and more—video works best when things are in motion.
- Think in terms of story structure. This happens, then this happens, then this happens, the end. Even the simplest video capture needs a beginning, a middle, and an end. A little bit of planning can have a big effect on the final product.
- All content exists for one of the following reasons: to educate, inspire, demonstrate, or entertain. A video can do more than one at the same time, but it will fail if it doesn't accomplish at least one.
- Diners are used to seeing the finished product, so take the time to show them something they don't often see. Find ways to let them in on the process.
- As the saying goes, "People buy from people," so find opportunities to put your team front and center. Video is a great medium for bringing their stories to life; this helps strengthen connections between the business, the staff, and the guests.
- I don't know how else to say this, so I'll just say it: get comfortable on camera. The best way to make your case is to say it in your own words directly to the people who matter. The world is digital and the opportunity to reach that world is literally at your fingertips. Practice, study, and ask for help when all else fails. Do whatever is necessary to get good in front of the camera.

AUDIO

- The power of audio is that it allows us to multitask. We can catch up on our favorite podcast while commuting to work . . . listen to our favorite songs while polishing silverware . . . learn something new while prepping dinner service. All of us are experts at consuming content, so don't let this powerful medium pass you by.

- You may not be good on video, but I bet you'd do just fine talking into a microphone for thirty minutes, especially if you found someone interesting to join you. Very few operators are using audio to help market their restaurant, and I think there is a huge opportunity just waiting to be exploited.

- Prep, don't script. Have a clear idea of what you'd like to say and the order in which you'd like to say it, but stay loose enough to let yourself go from time to time. If you're interviewing guests, simply ask questions that you want the answers to. Listen closely to their responses and let your curiosity guide the conversation.

- If you're going solo, remember that each piece of content needs to serve a specific purpose. Understand what you're trying to achieve with the episode and keep driving toward that goal. Always ask yourself, "What do I want people to come away with?"

- Take your time, catch your breath, and enunciate clearly. You don't have to be polished and perfect, but you're going to be in someone's ears, so you need to respect the intimacy of that connection.

- Show up with consistency and respect the time and attention of your listeners. Think of their needs and find ways to serve them generously and selflessly.

SMELL, TASTE, TOUCH

- Scientists often say that smell is the most powerful of the five senses. That's because our olfactory nerve is connected to the amygdala, which plays a key role in the way we experience memory. Building a connection between your restaurant and the guest can be greatly enhanced simply by understanding the power that smell has over us.

- Taste and texture are deeply connected. Crispy french fries are the perfect pair for a tender, moist burger. Toasted croutons add a desirable crunch to any Caesar salad. Lemon on fish. Butter on lobster. Mustard on hot dogs. You get my point. Use taste and texture to surprise (and delight) your guests.

- As humans we are hardwired to seek out safety. How we perceive the environment around us has a lot to do with our ability to find pleasure in that environment. This is obvious to a certain degree. It's why we dim the lights and place comfy chairs in our restaurants. Think of all the other ways you might be able to put your diners at ease.

- What are the things your diners will touch throughout their meal? The menu, wine list, silverware, wine glasses, napkins? What role does each of them play in communicating your brand promise? This may sound silly, but I promise it makes an impact to go this deep.

Trends are always changing, and so you need to stay current with best practices. There are incredible resources available on the internet—blogs, podcasts, websites, and more—dedicated to the art and science of creating good content. The list above simply outlines some of the fundamentals. They are less tactical, more strategic. Trends come and go, but the strategy behind creating smart, compelling content never will. My hope is that this chapter will stay relevant for a long, long time. I urge you to share these with your team and even add some of your own insights to the list.

ASSIGNMENT #18

I want you to take fifteen minutes and sign up for as many email lists as you can. Start with your competitors. You need to know what and how they're communicating with their audience. Look to other markets—restaurants you admire—and take the time to sign up for their lists as well. Inspiration can be found in many places.

Likewise, I want you to make sure you're following all your competitors on social media. Find other accounts you admire—again, restaurants in other markets, perhaps—and start following them as well. Check in every day or so to see how they're using the platform and see if there's anything you should be doing on your own accounts.

Visit websites and stop in at different restaurants in your neighborhood, simply to figure out what other people are doing to market their restaurants. Follow trends and find ways to keep up with best practices. You don't have to be cutting edge, but you need to be able to use the platforms in the most effective way possible.

PART FOUR
PUTTING IT
TOGETHER

CHAPTER 19

SYSTEMS AND GOALS

I work with clients all over the world, and the one thing they all have in common is the need for clear systems. In fact, it's one of the first lessons we cover whenever anyone comes into my mastermind program. Your job as an owner or operator is to get good at identifying problems, then prioritizing those problems. Before we start solving a problem, we need to set a goal. Do that well, and you're more than halfway home. But hold up! There's very specific criteria we use to set goals for our problems.

In 1981, George Doran, Arthur Miller, and James Cunningham published an article in *Management Review* titled "There's a S.M.A.R.T. Way to Write Management's Goals and Objectives." In it they identified an acronym—SMART—that could be used as a framework for managers to help motivate their teams. It stands for specific, measurable, assignable, relevant, and time-bound.[16] If we are to achieve anything, they argued, the parties involved need to agree on it before undertaking the project. Goals need to be set. But not just any goals . . . SMART goals.

To begin, they argued, you must make the goal SPECIFIC. If you make it specific, by default it becomes MEASURABLE. We also want to provide accountability, so we make it ASSIGNABLE. Next, we make sure our goal is RELEVANT to the success of the business. And finally, we must make the goal TIME-BOUND.

Goal setting is one of the most important pieces of building a successful business and marketing that business. But you may have noticed that the title of this chapter is "Systems and Goals." One cannot exist without the other. For example, even the SMART framework is itself a guideline for systematizing the way you and your team set goals. I'd like to take this one step further and invite you to build systems for every aspect of your restaurant.

We identify problems and prioritize those problems. Before we start solving those problems, we set goals for ourselves. We then must take action. To get from point A to point B, we are going to do the following things. When you write those things down, they become a repeatable set of actions. And if it's repeatable, it's scalable. Meaning, you can delegate those tasks to others; you can train others how to do what needs to be done. This is the only way to affect meaningful change, but guess what:

> **MINDSET SHIFT**
> If we want things to change, then we
> must be willing to change things.

You get started by looking at your current efforts to assess what's working and what isn't. Armed with that information, you can begin to set a course forward—a path to greater sales, for example.

To make this decision, you need to put a system into place. In this example, you need the following things:

1. A framework for assessing current efforts
2. A creative outlet for brainstorming new ideas
3. A way to determine which of those new ideas are worth pursuing
4. A process for successfully implementing those ideas

Do this correctly, and even if you fail to accomplish your stated goal, you will have identified a repeatable process—otherwise known as a *system*—for attempting to reach future goals. At the end of the designated time frame, you may not have hit your stated goal, but you may be able to say the following:

1. "We identified some weak points in our current efforts."
2. "We created a safe space where ideas could be tossed around and debated."
3. "We worked together to determine which of those ideas we should pursue."
4. "We took action and learned the best way to implement new ideas."

Simply wishing something so . . . does not make it so. You may want to increase revenue by 20 percent on Monday nights. Fine. And I'd like a hundred million dollars. But unless we take action, the two of us are just sitting around waiting for a miracle. Setting SMART goals is the first step and then building a system for change is the second. And, by the way, you don't have to follow the four-step framework I just laid out. You can do anything you want, just as long as it's specific and repeatable. Also, it's helpful if it fosters creativity, collaboration, and meaningful change within your organization.

To illustrate how this works in real life, I'll share an example from a few years back. I was working with a high-end restaurant here in New York City—a Michelin-starred property and one of the most popular restaurants in town. Summer was winding down, and we knew that sales always dipped between August 15 and September 15. Our regulars were always away on vacation; then they were always busy in the weeks following the Labor Day holiday as their children returned to school. We knew it would be hard to capture attention, but still we wanted to find a way to stave off the dip in sales we knew was coming.

I gathered the leadership team for an hour, during which we made sure everyone understood the problem we were trying to solve. We looked at revenue numbers from the past several years and made a projection about where we thought sales would be if we did nothing. We then applied the SMART goal framework to identify a tangible goal we could go after. In the end we came up with the following: "We want revenue in August and September to be 30 percent over last year's numbers." The next step was to figure out exactly how to do that.

Again, simply wishing it so will not make it so. And doing the same old things would not yield different results. So if we wanted a different outcome, we would have to pursue different actions. With the example I just shared, we spent a lot of time poring over the numbers, and ultimately those numbers influenced the ideas we brought to the table. In the end, we decided to develop a Late Summer Harvest Menu. This would be a set menu celebrating the flavors of the season (corn, tomatoes, beans, berries) and some of the local farms in the tri-state area. We chose to target a younger demographic (people who perhaps didn't have kids or vacation homes) at a lower price point (roughly 30 percent lower than our typical prices) on nights when they might not necessarily think to join us (Monday through Thursday).

And here's the last piece to this conversation about systems and goals: because we used a framework, then put a system in place for achieving those goals, we were poised to succeed even if we didn't accomplish our overall stated goal. When all was said and done, we actually didn't hit our goal of increasing sales by 30 percent, but we came close (24 percent). In addition, though, we also figured out a way to brainstorm ideas and put those ideas into practice. We developed a whole new menu and deepened the relationships we had with some of our beloved partners. Finally, we were able to identify, attract, and nurture a whole new demographic that, up until that point, we had never really been able to target. We tagged those guests in our system so that we could segment the list and speak to them with more specificity in future marketing campaigns.

In everything you do, I want you to figure out how you can make it a success, even if you fail to do the thing you set out to do. In this instance, our effort was rewarded, and despite missing that 30 percent mark, the project was deemed a success. Whether it's systematizing your inventory, developing a new spring menu, finding ways to save on labor, or brainstorming holiday promotion ideas . . . I want you to think strategically about what you're trying to do so that you'll succeed no matter what.

ASSIGNMENT #19

What are some systems you already have in place that work? Why do they work? What are some areas of the restaurant that could use clearer systems? What sort of process do you use in those instances? If there is no system, ask yourself why none exists. Make a list of everything—and I mean EVERYTHING—that needs to be systematized. BOH, FOH, hiring, firing, training, scheduling, menu development, floor management, marketing efforts, and so on.

The second piece is to figure out what your five biggest goals are right now for your restaurant. Write them down and then turn them into SMART goals. Now I want you to sketch out a plan—a system—for taking action. What needs to happen to make these a reality? Use the example from this chapter as a blueprint for going about it. Do it today.

CHAPTER 20

BUILDING A MARKETING PLAN

When I ask restaurant owners about their marketing plan, they'll often laugh and say, "We're just a small restaurant. We can't afford to do marketing!" And at this point in the book, hopefully you understand how wrong that statement is. If you sell products or services, you do marketing. If you rely on other humans to purchase those products or services, you do marketing.

MINDSET SHIFT
Everyone is a marketer; some are
just better at it than others.

One of the best ways to get good at marketing is to get organized. Since we've already established that you've got to "do marketing," you might as well put a plan in place that outlines everything you'll have to accomplish. The biggest companies in the world know this, and in my opinion, this is the dividing line between success and failure. Every business should have a marketing plan—a document that outlines what you're going to do, when you're going to do it, how it's going to get done, and why those efforts matter to the success of your business. But make no mistake, there is a right and wrong way to do this.

I've worked with hundreds of companies over my career and have helped many of them build marketing plans for their businesses. These documents can be ninety pages long (or more), but for everyone's benefit I'm going to show you how to create a marketing plan that is mercifully short—no longer than about fifteen pages. This will be an internal document, meant to communicate only the most pertinent details to your team. And—this is crucial here—it will be for a specific period of time. Meaning, you're going to build a marketing plan each quarter. At the end of that time, you'll do a fresh analysis of the market and your goals and then create a whole new document for the next quarter

Everyone builds their marketing plan a bit differently, but since this is my book, I'm going to show you how I like to do it. Specifically, this is a marketing plan for restaurants. You're certainly free to amend the structure as you see fit, just as long as it keeps your efforts focused and actionable. I like to divide up the document into seven different sections, each with a separate focus. Let me show you an efficient way to build an effective marketing plan.

———

SECTION ONE: THE PRODUCT, THE CHALLENGE, THE GOAL

Let's start by simplifying some things. What exactly are you offering? Meaning, what is the product, service, or experience you provide for your customers? Next, outline the challenge you face. Meaning, what stands in the way of you being as successful as you hope to be? Finally, then, outline the goal. What do you hope to achieve in the designated time period? If you overcome the stated challenge, what would success look like? You'd be surprised how effective this sort of specificity can be in getting your team onto the same page.

SECTION TWO: SITUATION ANALYSIS

All marketing plans include a situation analysis. In fact, it's usually the meat of the document, and because of that, I like to break this particular section down into five parts: market analysis, PEST analysis, internal analysis, external analysis, and finally, a SWOT analysis. This will give you a really good understanding of the world you're trying to enter. You'll have a clear idea of who you are and who you're for, all of which will help you craft a strategy for reaching your audience.

The market analysis is where we assess our market so we can understand how we might fit into it. You'll go through this systematically so that by the end, you've taken a 360-degree view. First up, you'll need to define your market. Literally, are we talking a region, a city, a neighborhood, or just a single block? The way you define your market will help you craft a strategy for entering that market.

Next you'll want to describe some of the demographics of that market. What are some of the pertinent details about the community you seek to serve? What's the median household income? How might that affect your ability to enter this market? What's the racial or ethnic makeup of the neighborhood? What sorts of restaurants are doing well in this market? How does all of that inform your decision to target this market?

Next you'll want to talk for a second about the current state of your industry. Are restaurants flourishing or struggling? What kinds of concepts are finding success? Why are the failing restaurants floundering? This will help you take the temperature of the water and build a concept that could succeed.

Talk about any recent developments in your market. Meaning, are there new houses being built, new businesses moving into the area? Is there nightlife that will help drive traffic or other restaurants that will help solidify the area as a destination for dining? A community is always in flux, and you simply want to understand what's happening in this one.

Specifically, then, you want to look back over the past year and peek forward just a year. What has happened recently, or what might happen in the near future? How has that affected your business? How might that impact business in the months to come? Once all of that is done, you're ready to move on to the second piece of the situation analysis.

PEST is an acronym that stands for political, economic, social, and technological. A PEST analysis is when you look at recent trends—globally or locally—that might affect your business. Just as you did earlier, I want you to go through each in a systematic way. What is happening politically in the world? Is there legislation being proposed that might impact your business? Is there a new administration on its way in? What might that mean for business?

Then look at the economic factors impacting your community. Is business booming, or are you fighting through a recession? What does the labor market look like? What does that mean for your ability to hire staff? And what does that mean for the community you seek to serve?

When we look at social trends, you want to consider what's happening with people's behaviors and buying habits. As I write this chapter, the world is emerging from the COVID-19 crisis, and social changes are on everyone's mind. Nearly 62 percent of employers now offer flexible workplace policies, allowing employees to work remotely at least part time,[17] and that is having a profound impact on urban and suburban markets. Convenience has been put front and center, and this is just what we're seeing today. We still have yet to feel the long-term effects of this pandemic. Undoubtedly you will be reading this at some point in the future, and the issues I just outlined will no longer be a concern to you. But I'm betting there will be new factors to consider. What are they?

Over the past thirty years, technology has played a key role in reshaping every major industry in the world. Think of the disruption it has caused to retail, travel, education, health care, publishing, music, film, and TV. Those same forces are at play in our industry as well, and things are changing at the speed of light. Your challenge is to identify the specific ways in which they're affecting your market and your business.

The next piece of any situation analysis is a look inward. An internal analysis is where you talk about the history of the company, the experience you provide, the people who make it happen, and where things currently stand. Luckily you did much of this work earlier when we were discussing the ABCDs of Marketing. Start there, then talk about revenue and check averages, and covers and growth forecasts. This is where you describe what's going on within the four walls of your restaurant—the good, the bad, and the ugly.

When you conduct an external analysis, really what you want to do is identify some of your key competitors. And again, you've already done this work, right? In the ABCDs of Marketing, C stands for Competition. So look back over that work and simply pull that information over here. But now, I want you to get a bit more focused. Narrow it down to your four or five biggest competitors, and describe the following things about them: their price, their communication strategy, and why a consumer might choose them over you. Do that for each and every one, and you should start to see how your competitors are positioning themselves in your market.

Finally, then, you'll want to create a SWOT analysis for your restaurant. SWOT is another acronym that stands for strengths, weaknesses, opportunities, and threats. The first two—strengths and weaknesses—are an internal assessment; the last two—opportunities and threats—are external. You start by looking at your company and identifying where you excel and where you're falling behind. Then you want to look at the world and identify opportunities you might be able to take advantage of and also risks that may or may not exist. This is where you pull together all the information in the situation analysis to craft direct statements about how you might succeed (or fail) in penetrating this market.

SECTION THREE: MARKET SEGMENTATION

This is where you start identifying your audience—literally the group you seek to serve. Sound familiar? It should. This is one of the first things we talked about early on in this book. Now I simply want you to identify three or four personas for your guests. The majority of your guests should be able to fit into one of those personas. Give each persona a name and find a picture online if it helps bring this exercise to life. (I always include pictures in my marketing plans for clients.) Then simply pull over all of the work you did in Assignment #2 when we discussed how to find your Audience. And don't forget about the pain point. Trust me, that last part is important—so don't skip it!

SECTION FOUR: THE MARKETING MIX

Remember the marketing mix is also referred to as the Four Ps, and they are product, price, place, and promotion. This is about as academic as I'll get here, but there is a reason these Ps persist after all these decades. What are you selling? How much does it cost? Where can people get it? And how do you communicate the benefits to your target audience? As I said earlier, I feel the 4P framework is a bit outdated, but if done right this single page can still pack a hefty punch.

SECTION FIVE: COMMUNICATION STRATEGY

Your company exists to solve a problem for a specific kind of person or for a specific group of people. Hopefully you've identified a compelling problem and have crafted a solution to that problem. Great! Now you just need to figure out how best to communicate that to the people you seek to serve. This is where you're going to map out a communication strategy.

First and foremost, let's get really clear on why a consumer would choose you over a competitor. What is the value you provide? What do you offer that they cannot get anywhere else?

How will you then communicate that visually? What colors and fonts do you use? What does your logo look like, and what does it say to a prospective customer? How else do you use design to tell your story? What does the physical space say about you? What about your website, business cards, posters, and postcards?

How would you describe the tone of your brand? What sort of imagery helps evoke that feeling? Literally, what should your images and videos look like, and how do they help tell the story? There should be a style guide so that any creatives you work with can quickly hook into the pillars of your brand.

Finally, then, it's time to think about your brand voice. How do you speak to your target audience? What tone of voice do you use? What sort of sentence structure? Are you serious or fun, cheeky or earnest, energetic or restrained? This is the voice you'll use on all written communications from social media captions to descriptions on your menu.

SECTION SIX: ACTION PLAN

No marketing plan would be complete without a way to put it all into action. Literally, you must take a second and acknowledge the following: What did you learn about yourself, your competitors, and your market—and how will you put those insights into practice? As I often say on the podcast, "Information is only as valuable as the action it inspires." For your action plan, I want you to remember the three sides to the Triangle Principle: Attraction, Retention, and Evangelism. Specifically, I want you to outline everything you're going to do to acquire new customers. Then I want you to outline the steps you'll take to bring those customers back. And finally, you must detail the ways in which you're going to inspire those customers to go spread the good word about what you're doing. Each piece should get its own page, and you need to clearly artic- ulate how you're going to succeed in each area.

SECTION SEVEN: STRATEGIC SUMMARY

All of that then brings us to the final section—just a single para- graph. The strategic summary should distill everything down to just a couple of key sentences. An executive should be able to flip to this last page of the document and get a clear idea of what you've got planned. This will force you to get laser focused about what you're doing, how you're going to do it, and why all of that should matter to a consumer.

ASSIGNMENT #20

Your job here is very simple: I want you to create a marketing plan for your restaurant using the structure I outlined in this chapter. It shouldn't take you more than a couple of hours, and I promise it will be well worth your time. To help, I'm sharing my Marketing Plan Template. You can download it for free by visiting TheRestaurantMarketingMindset.com/marketingplan.

CHAPTER 21
GETTING ORGANIZED

I n 1967 Charles E. Hummel published a short pamphlet titled *Tyranny of the Urgent,* and it can be summed up in this one simple observation he made: "Your greatest danger is letting the urgent things crowd out the important."[18] Understand that we always have a choice in where to put our focus, where to spend our time. Of course, we'd probably all agree that a hot dish should get served immediately to keep a guest happy, but that doesn't mean we have to sacrifice *everything* just to get it to the table in a timely fashion.

As an operator I know it's all too easy to get caught up in the daily crises we face. The busser is a no-show, your liquor delivery is late, the toilet in the women's bathroom won't stop leaking, and the guy on table twelve just sent back his food. Much of an operator's time is spent putting out fires, and to a certain degree that is unavoidable. But with a bit of forethought and planning, I want to show you how to attend to the urgent while still achieving your broader goals.

For me, it's as simple as getting organized. That begins with a good marketing plan that allows you to collect your thoughts and articulate your objectives to the team around you. But the true secret is to then build a comprehensive marketing calendar. This is a document—I typically create mine using Excel—that tracks all your activity across every single one of your channels. The document I use is thorough, and I'll happily share it with you. Simply visit TheRestaurantMarketingMindset.com/calendar to get the free download. For those who prefer to take the scenic route, I'm going to explain exactly how to make your own.

Across the top of the page, write "Marketing Calendar" followed by the year. This is going to track all your efforts for the next 365 days. You list the month in the first column, followed by the date, then the day of the week. After that you'll want a column to track important holidays or events throughout the year. Next to that you'll want to identify any promotions you might want to run (like Taco Tuesdays or Sunday Suppers). Every other column on this document should highlight a different marketing channel. Some examples would be email marketing, pop-up banners, Facebook, Instagram, TikTok, paid social, paid search, in-store collateral, radio advertising, and more. What you'll quickly realize by doing this exercise is just how many options are available to you and how much agency you have. It's reasonable to expect you might have ten or fifteen different marketing channels at your disposal.

This document should live in the cloud where everyone on the team can access it. That might mean Dropbox or Google Drive or any other cloud-based tool you prefer to use. Which platform you use matters less than actually using it!

Once the document is built, you'll want to start filling it up with details about the year ahead. An easy first step is to label each of the holidays throughout the year: New Year's Day, Valentine's Day, St. Patrick's Day, Passover, Easter, Mother's Day, Memorial Day, Father's

Day, Fourth of July, Labor Day, Halloween, Thanksgiving, Hanukkah, Christmas Eve, Christmas Day, and finally, New Year's Eve.

Some of these might be profitable days for you; on others you might decide to close the restaurant altogether. It's good to know that now so you can plan accordingly. For example, if you're closed on both Christmas Eve and Christmas Day, that accounts for two days of lost revenue in December. That should affect your sales projections, right? Take the time to drop all those holidays onto the calendar.

Next go ahead and label any other dates that might be important. For example, maybe you're a New Orleans–themed restaurant. If so, Mardi Gras is probably a big day, so it would make sense to add it to your calendar. Does your town do First Fridays or Saturday Street Fairs? What about Restaurant Week or other similar promotional events? Add them to the calendar.

Next you'll want to add in any other in-house promotions you typically run. For example, one of my clients does a Lobster Boil every Thursday night during the summer; another offers a Takeout Special on Monday and Tuesday nights in the winter months. Those would get added to the calendar along with any other sorts of promotions you think you might want to run.

Once that's done, you'll take a step back and look at the document in its entirety. What usually happens is that you'll start noticing gaps in your calendar. Think carefully about these times. Perhaps these are times when business is already good? Great! You don't need to do a thing. But what I usually find is that these gaps coincide with down times in business. Now is the time to gather your team together and start brainstorming some ideas. The beauty of the calendar is that it gives you a bird's-eye view of the entire year. At no other time will you be able to zoom out this far. And remember, you don't need to have all the answers right at this moment. If gaps remain, simply circle those dates and come back to them at a later point.

Once all the holidays, events, and promotions have been added to the calendar, it's time to start looking at your marketing channels. Again, what I hope you realize by looking at this document is that there are a lot of different ways you can promote your restaurant. Now you simply need to figure out the best use of your time and resources.

There is no one right way to do that. In fact, you will make mistakes along the way. You will misspend, waste money. It's inevitable. Embrace that and commit yourself to learning from whatever mistakes you do make throughout the year. The best way to learn is to make sure you're tracking your efforts. Remember what we discussed in Chapter 19: "What gets measured gets managed." The beauty of using a marketing calendar is that you get to see everything all in one place. Certain efforts should help you focus on Customer Acquisition, others should encourage Retention, and of course a portion of your efforts will be about promoting Evangelism among your guests.

Does this sound familiar? This is simply the Triangle Principle! All your marketing efforts should fall into one of those three areas. You just need to know which efforts are meant to be accomplishing which goals. And then, yes—you need to track the results.

You can do this any number of ways, but if you want my advice . . . this is what I would do. In fact, this is what I normally do with the clients I work with. Take the first few days of the year— literally January 1–3—and organize your calendar. Take the next few days—perhaps January 4–7—to figure out a budget. Literally, I want you to figure out what you will spend each and every month of the year on your marketing. At this point it doesn't matter what your budget is, just as long as you have one. (Though a good rule of thumb is to dedicate 3 to 4 percent to marketing.)

Now you know what you're going to do to promote your restaurant, and you have a rough sense of how much you're going to spend to accomplish your goals. Perfect! The next step is to get specific with your holidays, events, and promotions. Take the second week of the year—January 8–15—to figure out what you're going to do for every event, holiday, and promotion. In January you're going to plan out March through August, and in August you're going to plan out September through February. (Since Valentine's Day sort of marks the end of the holiday season, I recommend planning for it in August when you plan the rest of the major holidays.)

You're going to look at what you did the previous year and then make decisions about the year ahead. You're going to make data-driven decisions to help you plan future efforts. What sort of menu did you serve for Mother's Day last year? How much did you charge? How many guests did you serve? What was your total revenue captured on that day? What did your competitors offer? Were they more or less successful than you were? Armed with those answers, you can make a decision about what to do this year for Mother's Day. Set goals for the holidays that include covers and revenue. Make a plan for how to hit your goals!

You're going to do that for every single holiday and set deadlines for the team as to when decisions need to be made. For example, hopefully you're able to hold a series of meetings where leadership can gather together to make decisions on offerings, menu, and pricing. But after that, you'll need to delegate items to your team and set strict deadlines for them to follow. For example, when will you need the final menu? When will a press release need to go out? When will the reservation book open for this holiday? When will the website need to be updated with photos and descriptions?

Getting yourself organized is like starting with the ball on the fifty-yard line. You will have done something that most of your competitors won't even realize they should be doing. And you will put yourself in a much better position simply by taking a couple of hours to lay out your agenda for the year ahead. If there's one thing that will change your business overnight, this is it. Challenge yourself to be more deliberate about what you're doing. Your staff will notice. Your guests will notice. And before long it'll be obvious when you look at your monthly P&L statements.

ASSIGNMENT #21

Build your own marketing calendar and set aside a couple of hours *this week* to get yourself organized. Follow the blueprint I laid out in the chapter and then gather your team to set goals for the year ahead. And no, it doesn't matter when you're reading this. The best time to get started is NOW! Get yourself organized and watch as your business transforms before your very eyes. If you need help, I'm sharing my template. You can get it for free by visiting TheRestaurantMarketingMindset.com/calendar.

CHAPTER 22

OPERATIONAL SOLUTIONS

There's something I often tell my coaching clients: "All of our problems are marketing problems; they just can't be solved with marketing. Instead, they have to be solved operationally." There is a relationship between marketing and operations that is very easy to overlook. In fact, most restaurant operators never fully embrace it. Often it feels as if they go down the hall, build out a menu, sketch plans for the new restaurant, then deliver a binder full of information to the marketing team.

"Here, now go sell it," they seem to say, waiting for the marketing team to build the strategy that will magically sell the restaurant.

But that's not how a great business gets built—certainly not a great restaurant. In fact, in this example the operations team has missed something crucial; they've already begun building a product without first assessing the market to see if there's even a need for that product. Before long, they might wonder why the restaurant isn't hitting the forecasts they dreamed up while sipping coffee down the street. "Why aren't we busier?" The answer could have been found in those early meetings had they invited the marketing team to join the conversation.

The more productive way to build a business—as we talked about early in the book—is to work in reverse order. Instead of finding a customer for your product, it's far better to create a product for your customer. What would have happened had the marketers been invited to those early meetings? They could have identified a series of questions that first needed to be answered. Is there an unmet need in the market? Are we uniquely qualified to provide a solution to an existing problem? Could the solution we have in mind be more compelling than any of the alternatives out there? Only after these questions are answered can you begin the deep work of trying to deliver that solution to your audience.

In Part One of this book, I introduced you to the four-step framework I use with all of my clients; it's called the ABCDs of Marketing. This is where I invited you to figure out who in your market has a problem you might be able to solve. Then I asked you to go craft a solution to that problem. I encouraged you to figure out who else is trying to solve the same problem. And then finally, I asked you to differentiate yourself from the competition. This is a foundational piece that cannot be ignored.

So let's agree on this much: all great businesses begin by identifying a problem that needs to be solved. The product, service, or experience you then create should be the solution to that problem. Thought of another way . . .

MINDSET SHIFT

There is a relationship between
marketing and operations that must
exist for any restaurant to succeed.

And please note that relationship should be a dialogue.

It's the marketer's job to identify a target market and then figure out exactly what it is they need. Once that is identified, the operations team is tasked with developing a compelling solution to their problem. Knowing what the market wants and what kind of solution the operations team is crafting, the marketer can then work hard to communicate the product's value to the consumer. This, as it turns out, is pretty important. All transactions are a trade, where both the consumer and the merchant are giving something away. In the case of a restaurant, it's usually the customer giving money in exchange for a well-cooked meal. But remember, as we laid out earlier, there is much more being traded than just money and food. The merchant is also providing service, expertise, and aesthetics; the consumer is giving up time, attention, and trust.

We, as operators, must convince the consumer that what we're providing is more valuable than what we're asking for in return. Whether you realize it or not, this is the most important thing we do in our business: finding ways to communicate the value of what we provide. Of course, value is communicated in a variety of ways. Yes, some of that will be handled by the marketing team through copy and creative, but the experience itself should also be focused on creating value in the eyes of the consumer. Do you see how we just keep passing the baton back and forth between the marketing team and the operations team?

The food the chef chooses to serve and the prices she charges for that food will certainly influence the consumer's experience. But so will the lighting, music, decor, and service style. Even the way a chef decides to plate a given dish will have an effect on the dining experience, as will the font you use and the photos you choose to share on your company website. All of it communicates something to the consumer. And now—I hope you're realizing—we have come full circle. Remember back to the beginning of this book, I began by laying out the ABCDs of Marketing. And we learned that ABCD leads to E, and that E stands for *everything*. Every choice you make is an opportunity to communicate something important to a prospective diner. And too many restaurants struggle because they fail to realize that.

To put this into a more tangible example . . .

Let's say we're going to open a new restaurant. Our first step should be to survey the market. Literally we want to understand who we might serve and how they wish to be served. We look at the neighborhood and see who works in the area and who lives in the area. What are the demographics of the neighborhood? Can we learn something about consumer behavior? What other restaurants exist, and how are they performing? What types of restaurants don't yet exist in this market? Is there a reason they don't already exist? Has someone already tried and failed? If so, why did they fail? What does the market need that we're uniquely qualified to provide? Might they be open to something new? How might we introduce ourselves to the market?

This is the first job of every marketer—and no, you don't need a million-dollar budget. This can be something as simple as walking the street on a Tuesday night and peering inside the front window. Count the cars pulling in and out of the parking lot for the restaurant down the block; try to figure out—on average—about how many covers they get every day. See what's working in the neighborhood and try to figure out where there might be some white space in the market.

This is what we call market research, and if I'm being honest, it should be core to everything you do. Strange, right? Because here we are—nearly at the end of our time together—and I'm only just now bringing up a topic that I think is fundamental to your success. But see, I don't think we could have had this conversation before now. We needed to go a long way out of our way to come back to this. But listen carefully:

> **MINDSET SHIFT**
> Most restaurants struggle simply because
> they don't ask the right questions.

One of my professors in business school said something that still resonates with me: "You get better answers by asking better questions." Before you open a restaurant, you need to ask yourself a series of questions beginning with the obvious one: "What does the market need?" Then: "Is it possible to provide a compelling solution to the problem they have?"

Once you ask a question, you need to figure out the best way to get the answer you need. Each answer should lead to another series of questions. You set out to answer each question until you feel like you understand your market, your audience, and your competitors. The answers will help you craft a solution. The solution will eventually be your restaurant.

Market research is the way we find the answers to our questions and understand that there are many tools available to you. Sometimes simple observation is enough—sitting at the bar of the restaurant down the street, eavesdropping on conversations at the nearest coffee shop, watching what people do when they get their food, and observing their reactions when they get the final bill.

From there you might find that you need more than what you can easily observe. So maybe you invite diners to fill out a quick survey or you do a series of five-minute interviews at the mall down the street. The bottom line is that it begins by asking yourself a question. Then you can figure out the best way to go find an answer to that question.

At the end of this—and it could be two days, two weeks, two months—let's say you discover that the neighborhood could use a high-end fine-dining restaurant. Your marketing team needs to now begin a dialogue with the operations team to figure out a shape for this new establishment. Again, this is a dialogue. The constant back and forth is the only way this will work.

Now, undoubtedly many of you are probably following along and thinking, "Give me a break! I can't afford a marketing department. This business is just me at the moment." And that's fine. You simply need to learn how to switch hats. You need to be the marketer, then the chef, then the general manager, then the marketer again. People may think you're crazy, talking to yourself as you pore over menus—I don't care! Remember, there is a relationship between marketing and operations. Without it, the concept will fail, so get good at wearing many hats.

Before we leave this, I'll make one final point: the dialogue does not end once the restaurant opens. Consumer behavior will change over time—certainly we've all witnessed that over the past few years.

What your customers want will evolve, and how you reach them will constantly shift. The key is to maintain strong communication between marketing and operations. Continue to ask good questions and use those answers to better serve your audience. As marketers we should constantly strive to put ourselves in our customers' shoes. What is it they need? Understanding that will help you serve them in new and wonderful ways. And they will thank you by giving you their business and spreading the word about who you are and what you do. In time, your brand will grow simply because you are filling a need, solving a problem in a compelling way, which, in my mind, is what this business is all about.

ASSIGNMENT #22

I want you to take a blank piece of paper and think about the questions you need answered. It can start with something as obvious as: "Why aren't we busy on Monday and Tuesday nights?" Perhaps that then leads you to better questions like, "Where do my customers normally dine on those nights?" "Do they dine with my competitors or prefer to get takeout?" "Or maybe they prefer to cook at home those nights?" How might you go about getting the answers to those questions? Maybe your customers just don't think of you on those nights. Or simply need a bit more convincing to change their regular behavior. For now, just make a list of questions—and let each question lead you to other (better) questions. At the end, brainstorm some ways you might be able to get the answers you need. You will eventually do this once a month with everything from covers to check average, menu design to marketing budget. Have fun getting to know your people!

CHAPTER 23

CREATIVITY IS A RENEWABLE RESOURCE

You may not know this about me, but I went to theater school as an undergrad. It was a rigorous, conservatory-style program designed to train Broadway performers, and I loved every second of those four years. Upon graduation I moved to New York City and began my theatrical career. And it was fun for a while—until it wasn't.

From a very early age, it was pounded into me that I was an artist. And I'm grateful for that. Creativity runs through my veins. But like many of us, we have a vision in our heads of what an artist does. We picture painters, musicians, dancers, photographers, actors—the kinds of artists that get celebrated for their innate talent and carefully honed craft. But creativity is not reserved for the select few. In fact, my father is one of the most creative people I know. And though he would disagree with me for even suggesting it, I promise you it's true.

Growing up, I was presented with two very different ways to carve out a life. My father was an actuary, meaning he made his living assessing risk for Fortune 500 companies. Using tables and charts, he was able to forecast decades into the future as a way of helping organizations make better choices about how they invest in their people. I think we can agree that this is not the kind of job typically filled by an artist.

Compare that to my mother. Over the past forty years she's built no less than four successful businesses, using her skills as an artist, craftswoman, and designer. She created her own line of jewelry for a while, then clothing. She was a decorative painter and muralist for the better part of two decades. And all of that eventually led her to launch an interior design firm. On the surface, I think most people would agree that she was the creative one in the family.

And when I left home to pursue a career in the arts, most people assumed I took after my mother. And rightfully so. There is a fair amount of truth in that statement. She and I both share the entrepreneurial spirit. Like her, I have started multiple businesses since leaving school. We're visual, right-brained, outside-the-box thinkers.

A moment ago I told you that my artistic career was fun for a while—until it wasn't. My excitement started to flag when I realized much of what was required of me as a performer was fitting into someone else's vision—literally, sometimes someone else's clothes. Famous actors certainly have agency over the projects they pursue and the way their careers unfold, but most performers never reach that level. Like many others out there, I found myself stuck in a rut where I had very little say over the work I did or the collaborations I got to pursue. Suddenly my life in the arts didn't feel all that creative anymore. Meanwhile, I was becoming more and more entrenched in the food world. I was opening a new restaurant every year, working alongside some of the smartest creatives I had ever met. In many ways, my restaurant career was scratching that creative itch in a way that the theatrical world just couldn't. But back to my parents . . .

It would be unfair to characterize my mother as the sole creative, just as it would be foolish to ignore all the creative work that happens on a daily basis in the restaurant industry. Even the bookkeepers I've worked with over the past two decades excelled at using creativity to keep the doors open on new restaurants that just hadn't yet "found their audience." And this is when I began to think a lot more about the work my dad does with numbers—the sorts of problems he wrestles with day in and day out.

See, it all comes down to our definition of creativity. Which leads us to another important shift . . .

> ## MINDSET SHIFT
> Creativity is about solving interesting
> problems in bold new ways.

When viewed through that lens, I think it unlocks the creative spirit in most of the people I coach. Consider a new parent desperately trying to get their little one to stop crying. Think about all of the things they try: changing the baby, feeding the baby, rocking that baby to sleep, walking the halls, bouncing them on their shoulder, turning on music, winding up the mobile, and on and on. In her own way, a new mother is an artist, employing creativity over and over as she tries to soothe a fussy child.

My father works in defined benefits. Early in his career, big companies were still offering pensions to their employees. In time, though, those pensions were replaced by other products like IRAs and 401(k)s. The goal was the same: to offer a generous retirement package as a way of luring great employees to come work for the firm. Only the products had changed and thus the execution. When things change, we must change as well. My dad (and his entire industry) had to learn how to solve the same old problem in a bold new way. And the old ways (outdated products) eventually just weren't good enough anymore. To break through, creativity was required.

My father once argued with me about this, and so I asked him to just close his eyes and think back to his last week at work. I asked him to think of a problem he was presented with. "Why was it a problem?" I asked. "Because we couldn't figure out how to fix it," he replied. That's right. There were things he and his colleagues knew to do, but they weren't going to work in this situation. Why? "Because this instance was uniquely different from past instances." He was forced to use his head and think of a new solution. If that isn't creativity, I don't know what is.

In fact, this is what a stereotypical artist is also trying to do. The painter, for example, approaches the blank canvas as a new problem each and every time. She cannot simply repeat past successes, nor can she copy those who came before her, not if she wants to say something new. She—like the actuary, the designer, the chef—is simply trying to solve an interesting problem in a bold new way.

What I'm begging you to do is this: think of yourself as an artist. You solve interesting problems all day long by thinking outside the box—by bringing your insight, experience, and perspective to the table. And guess what? You will never run out of creativity. In fact, as the title of this chapter suggests:

MINDSET SHIFT
Creativity is a renewable resource.

Not only is it renewable, but your pool actually expands the more you use it. That's the incredible thing about creativity. But you've got to get your reps in. Just like building muscle mass at the gym, you've got to work out every day to help it grow. Once you get into the habit, though, you'll find it's impossible to stop.

Which begs the question: How exactly do we build up that muscle? By developing what's called *the creative habit*. Embrace the power of routine by setting aside time each day to identify problems and solve those problems. Make a habit of thinking outside the box and just watch what happens. This might be a weekly brainstorming session with your management team or just daily journaling. The mastermind group I run offers a perfect opportunity for this sort of thing. In time, the members of the group get really good at identifying problems and working with each other to come up with interesting solutions to those problems.

It begins, though, with you simply committing to the act. Even if you just set aside thirty minutes a week for deep thought, it's a start. In time, you'll be able to expand that to two sessions a week, then three, or four, or however many you find you need. Identify problems and challenge yourself to come up with bold, new solutions. That is how the world changes, how culture evolves and grows. In a matter of weeks, you'll be amazed at the changes you see—both in yourself and your business. When you make this sort of thing a habit, it becomes part of your daily routine—part of who you are. And I want you to embrace the creative genius I know you are. You just need to give yourself the space to find it.

ASSIGNMENT #23

Carve out thirty minutes today or tomorrow when you can lock yourself away in a quiet room without interruption. No creative work yet! In this thirty-minute session, I want you to open your calendar and set a regular routine for you to do this deep, creative problem-solving. Write out a contract and force yourself to sign it. It should go something like this:

I am committing myself to thirty minutes of deep, creative problem-solving every Tuesday morning from 9:30 to 10:00 a.m. and then a weekly brainstorming session with my team on Fridays from 3:00 to 3:30 p.m. I will maintain that routine for the next three months without interruption and then set a new schedule after that.

Do that and watch how your life changes.

CHAPTER 24

STEPPING AWAY

Something interesting happens when you start thinking of yourself as an artist. You'll begin to exert your creativity in the most interesting ways. You'll also start to inspire others, attracting those who believe what you believe. The collaborative spirit will become part of your culture, and I think you'll find that people will bring a sense of positivity to their work.

I've found that there are really only two kinds of people in this world: those who complain when something's broken and those who fix the thing when it breaks. I want you to create a culture where people show up with their toolboxes, understanding that every day will present a series of challenges that need to be fixed. You will learn to fix these problems to the best of your ability, drawing on the unique experiences you've had, using the various skills you possess. When you use your creativity, you become a force of positivity. And that, as it turns out, is a profound realization:

MINDSET SHIFT
Creativity breeds positivity,
and all that positivity will help inject a
sense of ownership into your staff.

This is perhaps the most important shift I want you to make because it is the true secret to running a profitable business. Your job as a leader is to invite your team to take ownership of the problems they face and empower them to find bold solutions to those problems. Give them the structures they need to be effective and then get out of their way so they can do what you hired them to do.

The cure to burnout is to learn how and when to step away. The only way that's possible is if you surround yourself with a strong team of Ambassadors who understand how to execute your vision and are driven to create the very best restaurant they can. By living your vision, they will create Evangelists for your brand. And that's how your business will rise to new levels you never thought possible.

In the end, I'm inviting you to create a business that works as hard as you do. By serving your market, you will become a pillar in your community, creating hundreds of jobs and feeding everyone around you. You have the opportunity to be a positive force for change and live the life you've always dreamed of.

And while some of you may have lofty ambitions of spreading your brand to the far reaches of the globe, I'm guessing that most of you have more humble aspirations. Most of the people I meet—the listeners who email me and the clients I coach—simply want to pursue their passion with a business that can consistently provide for their family. But to do that you need to build a business that operates efficiently without you.

I often tell my clients, "Your restaurant should not rely on any one person, whether that's the bartender, busboy, chef, or owner." Yes, that means you. I think it's irresponsible and dangerous. If you get hit by a bus, and the restaurant can't operate without you, you're literally letting down everyone around you. Your community expects to be fed by you. Your staff relies on these jobs so they can pay their bills. And your family relies on the profits you bring in to put a roof over their heads. Instead, I want you to start building an exit strategy.

If you got sick tomorrow and could not show up to work, what would need to happen for the business to operate without you? My guess is your restaurant would struggle if you suddenly couldn't show up, right? So challenge yourself to come up with an exit plan over the next thirty days.

Once that plan is on paper, you need to take steps to implement it. Once in place, you get to simply show up when you want. Best of all, when you're there, you can focus on all the other areas you've neglected up until now. In many ways, you'll finally be giving yourself the space to work *on* your business instead of just *in* it. And that's the last shift—the one that will change everything for you. It's an old cliché, but boy, oh, boy does it ring true:

> **MINDSET SHIFT**
> Restaurants succeed when their owners
> have the ability to work not just *in* their
> business, but *on* their business.

What I'm guessing is that you currently don't have the time to enact half of the suggestions in this book, and that's a wonderful problem to have. It's the first (and perhaps most important) problem we need to tackle. Write it down and start sketching out a plan to change it. Get creative. Think outside the box. And invite others into your circle. Task them with some of this and watch what collaboration does to your business.

Ours is a people business. We employ people, partner with people, buy from people, and sell to people. So let some of those people be part of the solution. On their own, John and Paul each had just a couple of chart toppers, but together they were responsible for twenty number-one hits with The Beatles. Two heads literally are better than one. So create the kind of place where that becomes obvious to both your patrons and your staff. As I said earlier, collaboration truly is one of the keys to building a successful business.

Remember that we take care of people for a living. We literally give them things that they put into their bodies. That requires empathy and trust. In a word, it is extraordinary, and make no mistake—not everyone could do it.

If you want to build a profitable restaurant, you need to put the people first. Your patrons and your staff, of course. Your family and friends, I hope. But finally—and perhaps most importantly—yourself. Solve interesting problems by serving people in bold, new ways. Bring originality to everything you do. And finally, build a life *you love* by showing others how to create a life *they love*. I promise you, it's the seasoning that gets sprinkled over every dish that comes out of your kitchen.

And yes, it does make everything taste better.

ASSIGNMENT #24

I want you to plan a two-week staycation. It must be in the next ninety days. Build a plan for your staff. What do they need to know to keep the restaurant running without you? What sort of training is needed? Checklists, prep sheets, closing paperwork, and so on? Who will handle ordering and inventory? What about scheduling? Put everything in motion and then stay out of the restaurant for two weeks.

You won't believe how your staff rises to the occasion. Do that, and your restaurant will change forever. Shortly after that your life will begin to change as well.

FAREWELL

It's never really goodbye, is it? Not in our industry, at least.

And yet, night after night, you have diners in your restaurant who will never, ever come back to dine with you. This, I'm sure, is something that causes you great pain. So I'm going to send you off with a little trick that will bring you closer to your guests and drive more repeat visits than anything else I've ever done. It's a game I teach my clients, one that I'm only too happy to show you. I can think of no better way to close this book.

Tonight I want you to try something. And I'll warn you, it's going to be more difficult than you can possibly imagine. For the entire night you cannot say the following line: "Thanks so much. Have a great night." Instead, you're going to replace that with one of the following lines:

"Thanks so much. When will we see you again?"

"Thanks so much. Can I make a reservation for you again next week?"

"Thanks so much. When are you coming back?"

I often do this game when I consult for fine dining restaurants.

Specifically, when I work with the maître d' or manager. They're so focused on hitting their marks—making sure everything is perfect—that they sometimes forget they are humans taking care of other humans. It becomes so easy to lose the hospitality. But when I force them to ask a fairly direct question like that, they become more present. Immediately they realize that they can't just come right out and ask people to book another reservation. They must do it with a wink and a smile. That moment requires charm and charisma.

But like I said just a moment ago, this little game works better than any other tactic I've developed. In fact, my clients consistently see a 20 percent close rate. And no, I'm not making that number up. So what have you got to lose, right? Yes, it requires you to be direct, but in the end, it will yield more covers. It will also help you build a more meaningful connection with the people you're serving. Both ultimately help create a better restaurant. Which is really what it's all about, right?

So I'll leave you with two challenges before I say farewell:

1. Play this game tonight in your restaurant. For an entire night, I want you to scrub that line from your vocabulary ("Thanks so much. Have a great night.") and replace it with something more direct, something that actually helps your business.

2. I want you to give this book to someone who's ready for it. That may be a partner, manager, or perhaps another restaurant owner across town. Help me spread these ideas because when one of us wins, we all win.

Cheers!
Chip

READING LIST

If there's anything I'm good at, it's taking vast amounts of information and distilling it down into simple, actionable frameworks. There are dozens of marketers and thought leaders who have inspired me over the past twenty years, and I am only too happy to share the love whenever I can. Below is a list of the thirty books I believe all restaurant owners should read.

- *Atomic Habits* by James Clear
- *Building a StoryBrand* by Donald Miller
- *Contagious* by Jonah Berger
- *Creativity, Inc.* by Ed Catmull and Amy Wallace
- *Customer Centricity* by Peter Fader
- *Delivering the Digital Restaurant* by Meredith Sandland and Carl Orsbourn
- *Drive* by Daniel Pink
- *Everybody Writes* by Ann Handley
- *Good to Great* by Jim Collins
- *Grit* by Angela Duckworth

- *Innovation and Entrepreneurship* by Peter F. Drucker
- *Jab, Jab, Jab, Right Hook* by Gary Vaynerchuk
- *Kitchen Confidential* by Anthony Bourdain
- *Marketing Rebellion* by Mark Schaefer
- *Originals* by Adam Grant
- *Positioning: The Battle for Your Mind* by Al Ries and Jack Trout
- *Post Corona* by Scott Galloway
- *Primalbranding* by Patrick Hanlon
- *Purple Cow* by Seth Godin
- *Setting the Table* by Danny Meyer
- *Start with Why* by Simon Sinek
- *The Art of Possibility* by Rosamund Stone Zander and Benjamin Zander
- *The Bullhearted Brand* by Joseph Szala
- *The Elements of Style* by William Strunk and E. B. White
- *The Inevitable* by Kevin Kelly
- *The Ministry of Common Sense* by Martin Lindstrom
- *This Is Water* by David Foster Wallace
- *To Sell Is Human* by Daniel Pink
- *Tribes* by Seth Godin
- *Unreasonable Hospitality* by Will Guidara

NOTES

1   Rory Crawford, "Restaurant Profitability and Failure Rates: What You Need to Know," *FSR,* April 2019, https://www.fsrmagazine.com/expert-takes/restaurant-profitability-and-failure-rates-what-you-need-know.

2   United States Census Bureau, "QuickFacts New York City," last updated July 1, 2021, https://www.census.gov/quickfacts/newyorkcitynewyork.

3   Stephen Sondheim, *Finishing the Hat* (New York: Alfred A. Knopf, 2022), Preface, xv.

4   Simon Sinek, *Start with Why* (New York: The Penguin Group, 2009), 37.

5   "Transaction," Oxford English Dictionary, Google, accessed February 10, 2022. https://www.google.com/search?q=transaction&source=hp&ei=agu-JY4LwBtCy5NoPsP-iwAQ&iflsig=AJiK0e8AAAAAY4kZejaYR7pAiBoI-HG0KPmkWD65QZDGd&ved=0ahUKEwiCza-Tntn7AhVQGVkFHbC_CEgQ4dUDCA8&uact=5&oq=transaction&gs_lcp=Cgdnd3Mtd2l6EAMy-CAgAEIAEEELEDMgsIABCABBCxAxCDATILCAAQgAQQsQMQgwEyCA-gAEIAEEELEDMgUIABCABDILCAAQgAQQsQMQgwEyCAgAEIAEEELED-MggIABCABBCxAzILCAAQgAQQsQMQgwEyBQgAEIAEOhEILhCABB-CxAxCDARDRAzoICC4QsQMQgwE6DgguEIAEEELEDEMcBENE-DOgsILhCABBCxAxCDAToLCC4QgAQQxwEQ0QM6BQguEIAEOggIAB-

CABBDJAzoHCAAQgAQQClAAWM8LYOMNaABwAHgAgAE_iAG3B-JIBAjExmAEAoAEB&sclient=gws-wiz.

6   "Value," Oxford English Dictionary, Google, accessed November 9, 2022. https://www.google.com/search?q=value&ei=bQuJY-ikFv-Syt-MP2tWU2A4&ved=0ahUKEwioj_aUntn7AhV_iXIEHdoqBesQ4dUD-CBA&uact=5&oq=value&gs_lcp=Cgxnd3Mtd2l6LXNlcnAQAzII-CAAQsQMQkQIyBQgAEJECMgoIABCxAxxCDARBDMgoIABCxAxxC-DARBDMgsIABCABBCxAxxCDATIECAAQQzIICAAQgAQQsQMyBQ-gAEIAEMgQIABBDMggIABCABBDJAzoUCC4QgAQQsQMQgwEQx-wEQ0QMQ1AI6EQguEIAEELEDEIMBEMcBENEDOggILhCxAxxCDA-ToLCC4QgAQQxwEQ0QM6DgguEIAEELEDEMcBENEDOgcILhCx-AxBDOgsILhCABBCxAxxCDAToLCC4QsQMQgwEQ1AI6FAguEIMBEMc-BELEDENEDEJECEOoEOggILhCABBCxAzoRCC4QgAQQsQMQgwEQx-wEQrwE6BQgAELEDSgQIQRgASgQIRhgAUABY4wNg6AdoAHAAeA-CAAVmIAfgCkgEBNZgBAKABAcABAQ&sclient=gws-wiz-serp.

7   "About Niman Ranch," Niman Ranch, accessed December 15, 2022, https://www.nimanranch.com/about-niman-ranch/.

8   Gretchen Rubin, "Chef triumphs over tongue cancer and in the culinary world," UChicago Medicine, October 9, 2019, https://www.uchicagomedicine.org/forefront/cancer-articles/chef-triumphs-over-tongue-cancer-and-in-the-culinary-world.

9   "The Paris Tasting," Grgich Hills Estate, accessed January 5, 2023 https://www.grgich.com/the-paris-tasting/.

10   Kathi Kruse, "Rule of 7: How Social Media Crushes Old School Marketing, September 29, 2021. https://www.krusecontrolinc.com/rule-of-7-how-social-media-crushes-old-school-marketing-2021/

11   Joseph A. Schumpeter, *Capitalism, Socialism and Democracy* (New York: Harper Perennial, 1942), 82-83.

12   "Top websites," Semrush, accessed March 10, 2023, https://www.semrush.com/website/top/.

13   Alexandra Twin, "The 4 Ps of Marketing and How To Use Them in Your Strategy," *Investopedia*, last updated December 14, 2022, https://www.investo-pedia.com/terms/f/four-ps.asp.

14   Seth Godin, *Seth's Blog.* January 31, 2008. https://seths.blog/2008/01/permission-mark/.

15   Kevin McSpadden, "You Now Have a Shorter Attention Span Than a Goldfish," *Time*, May 14, 2015, https://time.com/3858309/attention-spans-goldfish/.

16   G. T. Doran, "There's a S.M.A.R.T. Way to Write Management's Goals and Objectives," *Management Review* 70 (1981), 35–36.

17   Owl Labs, "State of Remote Work 2022," https://owllabs.com/state-of-remote-work/2022.

18   Charles E. Hummel, *Tyranny of the Urgent* (InterVarsity Christian Fellowship of the United State of America, 1967), 1.

ABOUT THE AUTHOR

Chip Klose is a New York City–based restaurant coach as well as the host of the *Restaurant Strategy* podcast. He's amassed more than two decades of operational experience in the hospitality industry, opening Michelin-starred restaurants and collaborating with numerous James Beard Award–winning chefs. He is a contributing writer for *Bar & Restaurant* and travels the country as a noted public speaker, giving presentations on marketing, operations, technology, and more. He earned his MBA in food marketing from Saint Joseph's University, where he frequently teaches as a guest lecturer.